ADORING THE SAINTS

THE WILLIAM & BETTYE NOWLIN SERIES
in Art, History, and Culture of the Western Hemisphere

# ADORING THE SAINTS

## *Fiestas in Central Mexico*

YOLANDA LASTRA, DINA SHERZER,
AND JOEL SHERZER

UNIVERSITY OF TEXAS PRESS

*Austin*

Copyright © 2009 by the University of Texas Press
All rights reserved
Printed in the United States of America
First edition, 2009

Requests for permission to reproduce material from
this work should be sent to:
Permissions
University of Texas Press
P.O. Box 7819
Austin, TX 78713-7819
www.utexas.edu/utpress/about/bpermission.html

∞ The paper used in this book meets the minimum requirements of
ANSI/NISO Z39.48-1992 (R1997) (Permanence of Paper).

Library of Congress Cataloging-in-Publication Data

Lastra, Yolanda.
Adoring the saints : fiestas in central Mexico / Yolanda Lastra,
Dina Sherzer, and Joel Sherzer. — 1st ed.
p. cm. — (The William & Bettye Nowlin series in art, history, and
culture of the western hemisphere)
Includes bibliographical references and index.
ISBN 978-0-292-72575-1
1. Fasts and feasts—Mexico—San Luis de la Paz.  2. Fasts and feasts—
Mexico—San Miguel de Allende.  3. Christian patron saints—Mexico—
San Luis de la Paz.  4. Christian patron saints—Mexico—San Miguel de
Allende.  5. Louis IX, King of France, 1214–1270—Cult—Mexico—San
Luis de la Paz.  6. Holy Week—Mexico—San Miguel de Allende.
7. Chichimeca-Jonaz Indians—Mexico—San Luis de la Paz—Religion.
8. Chichimeca-Jonaz Indians—Mexico—San Luis de la Paz—Social life
and customs.  9. Otomi Indians—Mexico—San Miguel de Allende—
Religion.  10. Otomi Indians—Mexico—San Miguel de Allende—Social
life and customs.  11. San Luis de la Paz (Mexico)—Religious life and
customs.  12. San Miguel de Allende (Mexico)—Religious life and
customs.  I. Sherzer, Dina.  II. Sherzer, Joel.  III. Title.
BX1428.3.L37 2009
263′.98097241—dc22
2009006975

# CONTENTS

ADORING THE SAINTS

# INTRODUCTION

Latin America is well known for its exuberant festivals and rituals. These include indigenous curing and puberty rites, Mardi Gras and carnivals, and town and village patron saint fiestas. While derived in part from ritual observances of the Catholic Church, Latin American fiestas typically commingle European, indigenous, and African elements. They are a centuries-old way of letting off steam, celebrations that are simultaneously sacred and profane, hegemonic and counter-hegemonic, serious and playful. They are an intense expression of identity and ethnicity, a celebration of historical and religious events, a release of personal and social energy, and a display of popular aesthetics. They are occasions for time off and time out from everyday behavior. Latin American fiestas are found in indigenous communities, ones of European origin, and African diasporic communities. They involve many modes of communication and sensory expression—verbal, nonverbal, visual, auditory, gustatory, olfactory.

This book looks at a widespread type of fiesta, the fiesta in honor of the patron saint of a place. We study the Central Mexican patron saint fiestas of Holy Burial (*Santo Entierro*) in Cruz del Palmar and Saint Louis (*San Luis Rey*) in San Luis de la Paz. These two communities are both situated in the state of Guanajuato. Cruz del Palmar is a small village near San Miguel de Allende, and San Luis de la Paz is a medium-size town eighty miles away. Our decision to study these two communities was not a random one. We discovered that people living in them, descendants of two distinct indigenous groups, the Otomi in Cruz del Palmar and the Chichimecs in San Luis de la Paz (called Chichimeca Jonaz, or Jonaces in appendix A2), are linked ritually through the historical circumstances their fiestas celebrate. Each community honors the other's saints and each participates in the other's patron saint fiesta, even though they are not in the same parish. Their participation in each other's fiestas is more than a simple visit to the saints, common enough among neighboring communities in this region at fiesta time. The special link between Cruz del Palmar and San Luis de la Paz as manifested in their saint's day celebrations is a central concern of this book, along with the specific activities, behaviors, and ritual objects that are customary to mandatory in the celebration of a patron saint.

Scholars have studied several aspects of patron saint fiestas in the region around Cruz del Palmar and San Luis de la Paz. These aspects include the spectacular dances and dance dramas, patterns of dances and costumes, and certain historical information.[1] Other scholars have examined the social function of patron saint fiestas and their place in popular religion.[2] While these studies are informative, there exists no published, comprehensive description of all the components of a fiesta. Through detailed observation of and participation in numerous patron saint fiestas, we came to realize that many specific elements are necessary for their conduct. In fact, a rigorous protocol is usually followed. There must be vigils (*velaciones*), masses, ritual blessings and cleansings (*limpias*), processions, dances or dance dramas, music, fireworks, ritual meals, and the ritual handling of special objects and flowers, all organized by confraternities consisting of specialists and officials (*cargueros*), led by ritual leaders (*mayordomos*), and with the participation of men, women, and children of all ages. Thus, a major contribution of this book is the detailed description, from an ethnographic perspective, of all activities, aspects, and moments of fiestas and the relationships among them. It is only through these descriptions that the significance and importance of the patron saint fiesta for the community and its culture can be broached. Moreover, it became evident that elements of Otomi, Chichimec, Aztec, and Apache cultures are juxtaposed and intertwined with Spanish and Mediterranean practices.

The various activities of patron saint fiestas are performances, and we study them as such. We have observed all of the special occasions on which people perform specific acts, such as speechmaking, singing, dancing, acting, playing instruments, reciting blessings, and cleansings, in particular contexts and places. During these performances individuals carry out assigned roles according to ritual kinship, knowledge, age, and gender. They wear special clothing and costumes and construct and display objects used only on the occasion of patron saint fiestas. They use their own language, a version of local, rural Spanish, with its own specialized and ritual forms of discourse and vocabulary and its own rhetorical and poetic features. Patron saint fiestas involve elaborate stagings, rituals, and theatricality, each with its own intrinsic aesthetics. These performances are sometimes private and intimate, sometimes public and collective. They vary widely in purpose and tone. They may be performances of religiosity and spirituality. They may involve boisterous movements of crowds. Often they are displays of ethnicity and of the memory and history of the community as the participants imagine it. We have recorded the actions and voices of participants in their own setting and language, and these appear in the book, transcribed, translated, and photographed.

Thus, our aim is a scholarly ethnographic study that renders the dynamism and creativity of patron saint fiestas, their visual, aural, kinetic, and verbal features, to convey the flavor and taste of these fiestas. In large view, we examine Mexican popular Catholicism through the lens of the fiesta and the fiesta through the lens of Mexican popular Catholicism. We describe each moment of the two fiestas in detail in order to capture their spirit, atmosphere, and purpose, but also to convey the rich sensory experience, the ritual performances, the texts used, and the beliefs that contribute to the simultaneously religious and profane mood of these events.

Along with this descriptive focus we offer an interpretation of fiesta activities in terms of the social, cultural, religious, and symbolic systems at work in them. We discuss the significance of the fiesta for the people and communities involved. We explore whether the fiesta activities are expressions of resistance, subversion, or affirmation of the participants' culture, beliefs, and identity. We examine what this popular religion represents and its relationship to official religion. We raise the question of whether fiestas involve a fusion of the Catholic and the indigenous religions, with a gradual diminution of the indigenous influence, or whether fiestas are Catholic interpretations of Indian rituals or indigenous interpretations of Catholic rituals. And we ask, who conquered whom? Did the Spanish Catholics conquer the Indians or did the indigenous forms win out and, in a sense, conquer the Catholic ones?

There is a specific aesthetic to the fiesta that has been barely mentioned by observers. For us, this popular and religious aesthetic, characterized by loudness, boisterousness, color, movement, and uncanny juxtapositions, is an essential element of the fiesta, and we spend some time on it. We also argue that the fiestas are traditions that were originally invented and now are reinvented and transformed, in a continuous process of creation, and that they have much to say about the identity of their participants in terms of their origins, their present-day situation, and Indian nation-state relationships in Mexico today.

Our understanding of fiestas draws on the extensive theoretical, methodological, and descriptive literature on fiestas and rituals and popular religion. We have benefited from reading studies in anthropology, history and ethnohistory, folklore, ethnomusicology, dance, religion, and Mexican national and popular culture. These studies include the following:

• The anthropology, history, and ethnohistory of Mexico and religion in Mexico, including notions of hybridity, syncretism, and *mestizaje* (racial and cultural mixture).[3]

• Studies of indigenous religions in Mesoamerica, in particular in Central Mexico.[4]

• National culture studies, which examine the expression of the Mexican national character as manifested in various phenomena, such as fiestas.[5]

• Functionalist studies, which describe in socioeconomic terms the function of fiestas (and popular religion more generally) for particular communities, the nation, and the world.[6]

• Symbolic and interpretive anthropology, which aims at a thick and deep description of cultural phenomena in the language of symbols, actions, and events.[7]

• Studies that see cultural phenomena such as fiestas as the locus of the continual construction, invention, and reinvention of traditions.[8]

• Studies of resistance, which see in fiestas and popular religion hidden transcripts of resistance to official, orthodox religion, conquest and conversion, Spaniards, the Mexican nation-state, and the global world system.[9]

• The discourse-centered approach to culture, which considers forms of discourse and communication—speeches, talking, gestures, music, dance, other performance forms—in relation to their social and cultural context.[10]

• A regional comparative approach, which examines other patron saint fiestas in Mexico for the light they may shed on the Cruz del Palmar and San Luis de la Paz fiestas.[11]

One of the many pleasures we have had carrying out the research for this book has been reading the wonderful scholarship on patron saint fiestas.

Each of these various perspectives sheds a different light on patron saint fiestas and gives us a different angle from which to interpret their complex meanings. Indeed, the complexity of fiestas requires multifaceted theoretical approaches. A single theoretical approach, no matter how pertinent, could only result in an impoverished and superficial description of complex, multilayered phenomena.

Central Mexico, and Mexico more generally, have attracted, fascinated, and challenged historians, philosophers, artists, writers, and anthropologists because of the rich complexity of culture, religion, and history and the intriguing question of how this complexity emerged and continues. We are contributing to this tradition and feel that this book about patron saint fiestas will be of interest to people wanting to know about popular culture and religion in Mexico, and about the fashioning and display of ethnicity and the invention and reinvention of traditions that take place in the fiestas.

With their prehistoric and historic, ethnic, religious, and sociocultural complexity, the patron saint fiestas of Cruz del Palmar and San Luis de la Paz reflect in many ways the heart and the symbolic and deep expression of Latin America. These fiestas are elaborate, expensive, complicated, comprehensive, local, national, international, traditional, constructed, and imagined. There is something for everyone. They are cultural performances and forms of communication. As Latin America becomes more and more industrialized and globalized, patron saint fiestas become more and more the sites for local and individual expressions of opposition and resistance to all this and adherence to more traditional, sometimes ancient (if still evolving) forms of symbolism and play. In all their varied moments, patron saint fiestas are an expression of the philosophy, theology, wisdom, vision of history, and perception of the Spanish conquest that participants have, presented in their own way and through their eyes, ears, and voices.

The collaborative fieldwork to document these two fiestas began in 1997. Yolanda Lastra, who had been carrying out linguistic research on the Otomi language in Cruz del Palmar and the Chichimec language in San Luis de la Paz, became aware of the two fiestas and the mutual participation of the communities.[12] She invited Dina and Joel Sherzer to join her in the study of these multiday, multi-event fiestas, when men, women, and children work together to honor their patron saints. This research has been a fascinating and thought-provoking experience, taking us centuries back in time and providing us with a new understanding of the present and of the heart of "deep Mexico" (*México profundo*).[13]

Over the years of our involvement in the patron saint fiestas of Cruz del Palmar and San Luis de la Paz, as well as other fiestas and religious activities in the region, we have come to know and appreciate the people, their rich lives, and their cultural practices, in particular their religious practices and celebrations. We have learned from their intellectual acumen and articulateness, their self-estimation, and their knowledge of their traditions. We have established wonderful relationships with many talented individuals. Those persons whom we came into contact with, those whom we interviewed, those with whom we spent days and nights observing and participating in their activities always greeted us with open arms, made us feel welcome, and were forthcoming in explaining what they were doing. They encouraged, indeed expected, us to record their fiestas on audiotape, videotape, and film. They clearly viewed themselves as collaborators in a project to document and interpret their fiestas.[14]

Since 1997 the three of us, together or separately, have observed different moments of both these fiestas. In addition, we were able to observe patron saint and related fiestas in surrounding villages and towns, including El Pueblito, La Ciénaga, La Cieneguita, Pantoja, Querétero, and San Miguel de Allende and its neighborhoods of Valle del Maiz, La Palmita, Guadiana, and Las Cuevitas, which share many features with those of Cruz del Palmar and San Luis de la Paz, as well as with fiestas elsewhere in Latin America and in Europe, particularly Italy and Spain. The cult of the saints, which was introduced to the New World from Mediterranean Europe, where it is still very much alive, flourished and is highly significant in the lives of the people who believe in it and practice it today. The vitality and continuity of these practices are the subject of the rest of the book.

# ONE

# SETTING THE STAGE

## CRUZ DEL PALMAR AND SAN LUIS DE LA PAZ

Along the main highway between San Miguel de Allende and Guanajuato, a sign at the entrance of a wide dirt road indicates Cruz del Palmar. This road takes one down several kilometers to this village (*rancho*), a parish (*parroquia*) belonging to the diocese of Celaya, and part of the municipality (*municipio*) of San Miguel de Allende. Cruz del Palmar can also be reached following the route of the seventeenth- and eighteenth-century chapels (*ruta de las capillas*) through several villages, from Atotonilco, a major religious center, to Cruz del Palmar. These villages—Banda, San Isidro de Banda, Montecillo de Nieto, and Oaxaca, as well as Cruz del Palmar and Atotonilco—were established at the locations of Otomi settlements. They constitute a tight network of communities and collaborate with one another during patron saint fiestas, contributing musical groups, dance groups, and ritual specialists. The communities attend each other's fiestas and pray for each other's saints. The chapels are still in use and are regularly maintained. The route is still actively visited by the faithful. The importance of Cruz del Palmar over time in this complex of villages may explain why it has such a long and elaborate festival today.

Cruz del Palmar is situated in a semi-arid desert landscape with rolling hills and a particular grouping of plants, several of which are important in the village's patron saint fiesta. These include desert spoon (*cucharilla*), a desert palm that looks somewhat like a maguey or agave cactus; mezquite; huisache (*huizache*), whose yellow puff-ball blooms provide the only note of color on the dry central plateau in January and February; the widespread prickly pear cactus (*nopal*); another widespread cactus, *garambullo;* organ cactus (*órgano*), cultivated as fences almost everywhere in drier climates; *carrizo,* a large reed; the pepper tree (*pirul*), a popular shade tree with feathery leaves and pink or red berries; and quince (*membrillo*), which is cultivated.[1]

Above the village of Cruz del Palmar, on a high hill, stands a chapel called the calvary (*calvario*). (Typically a calvary is a chapel-like construction erected on a hill and containing a representation of the crucifixion in the form of a cross, statue, or painting. A calvary may also be a shrine, or simply a cross at the side of the road or elsewhere.)[2] The calvary is built on a mound locally called a *cuicillo*. These mounds, frequent in the region, often contain ancient artifacts and are considered sacred. The calvary plays a central role in the patron saint fiesta in Cruz del Palmar. According to one ritual leader, it dates back to 1799. It is an intimate chapel whose walls are decorated with simple, stylized biblical scenes.

Cruz del Palmar, like many such villages in Mexico, has land owned communally (*ejido*). People raise corn, beans, and squash—the basic Mesoamerican vegetables—as well as other vegetables such as onions and cabbage. They also raise goats and sheep and a few cows, chickens, pigs, rabbits, and turkeys. Children can be seen riding donkeys, while men and women on horseback pass by on their way to buy or sell products. People own pickup trucks with either Mexican or U.S. license plates, and huge delivery trucks transport gravel extracted from a nearby quarry. Bicycles are also common. People wear traditional straw hats; younger men wear caps and boots and sometimes have cell phones on their belts. The village has a rodeo (*jaripeo*) arena dug into the ground.

The main road into Cruz del Palmar leads to the square, which has a central kiosk and benches, surrounded by stores, a health center, and schools (kindergarten, primary, and secondary). On one side of the square stands the parish church, which inhabitants proudly call the parroquia. The parish church and its atrium with its benches, a cross on the left side of the entrance to the church, and a small calvary (*calvarito*) on the right are central to the activities of the fiesta. The main part of this little church with whitewashed facade, bell tower, and dome is several hundred years old, with more recent additions. Just off the square are the remnants of an older chapel. Behind the parish church a street with a few stores leads to a path bordered by eucalyptus trees, then crosses a dry riverbed and rises slightly as it makes it way through fields. This is the place where, for as long as people can remember, the visitors from San Luis de la Paz have arrived to take part in the celebration of Holy Burial (Santo Entierro) and are met in a ritual encounter by the hosts of Cruz del Palmar and the entire population (see chapter four).

Streets are lined with houses, some of which are prosperous two-story buildings recently constructed or under construction. More often the houses are humble, one-story constructions with a dirt floor. Most houses have a small garden and an interior patio with trees and flowers. Some families have fields behind their houses where they grow such crops as corn, squash, and beans. All houses have electricity and television. Several large grocery stores in town sell fruit, bread, rice, beans, beer, canned food, some clothes, and pottery. Many families sell sodas and snacks from one of the windows of their house. People buy fresh tortillas in a tortilla store (*tortillería*) in the center of the village. Women earn money for their families by selling tortillas and vegetables in the San Miguel market. The village is growing in size; it is clean and well-kept. Economically, while not rich, it does not appear overwhelmed by poverty, no doubt because of an infusion of money from immigrants to the United States and from commerce with San Miguel. The day of the fiesta in Cruz del Palmar for the patron saint Holy Burial is January 1.

San Luis de la Paz was founded on August 25, 1552, as a defensive town to protect the silver that was being transported from Zacatecas to Mexico City.[3] Situated about eighty kilometers northeast of San Miguel de Allende, it is a prosperous commercial town also in the state of Guanajuato. Set in the middle of an agricultural region, San Luis de la Paz is intimately linked to its agricultural and ranching surroundings and is a bustling, active, and growing commercial center, with modern stores, government offices, banks, hospitals, bus stations, restaurants, hotels, bars, and a bullring (*plaza de toros*). The town has clean, paved streets, many well-kept shops, and tidy squares and parks with trees and flowers. There is a sense of order. It is a business town, not a tourist attraction. San Luis de la Paz has several churches and chapels, two of which are most important to the August fiesta, the parish church of San Luis de la Paz (parroquia de San Luis Rey) and the church of San Luisito (templo de San Luisito). San Luis de la Paz holds various festivals and fairs that attract many visitors to the area. A regional cultural, agricultural, and ranching fair in honor of San Luis takes place from August 10 to 26; the high point is the San Luis fiesta on August 25.[4]

Just east and almost touching San Luis de la Paz, the rural neighborhood of La Misión de Chichimecas is inhabited mostly by Chichimec Indians. La Misión is reached in several ways. In addition to two paved roads, one can reach La Misión by going up a dirt road from San Luis de la Paz to an area lined with houses, where people dry beans and husk corn in their yards. This dirt road is used for religious processions going to the center of San Luis. In the 1970s a paved road was built dividing La Misión into two sections, Upper Misión (Misión de Arriba) and Lower Misión (Misión de Abajo). Upper Misión is farther away from San Luis de la Paz and is more traditional; Chichimec is widely spoken. Lower Misión is more urbanized, and the Chichimec language is rapidly being displaced by Spanish.

La Misión does not have a central square with a church or official buildings. Its unpaved streets are lined with adobe houses, each typically with a central patio and a small garden. It has an official government medical clinic, a traditional medicine center, several chapels, several schools, and a few stores. People have electricity and television, but it is extremely poor and barren, especially when compared with the rest of San Luis de la Paz or with Cruz del Palmar. The economic status of the people is definitely quite low. A neighborhood of San Luis de la Paz near La Misión, San Ignacio, plays an important role in the fiesta. It is the place where the people of Cruz del Palmar arrive to celebrate Saint Louis with the inhabitants of La Misión and San Luis de la Paz and where a ritual encounter between the two communities takes place. In the San Ignacio chapel various fiesta activities occur as well. August 25 is the date of the fiesta for Saint Louis, the patron saint of San Luis de la Paz and La Misión.

How are the Chichimecs from San Luis de la Paz and the Otomi from Cruz del Palmar related? Why do they honor their respective saints and celebrate their respective patron saint fiestas together? Archaeological and ethnohistorical studies document the presence of Chichimecs and Otomis, along with other indigenous groups, in Central Mexico before the arrival of the Spaniards (see appendices A1 and A2).[5] The Chichimecs were hunters and gatherers who fought the Spaniards. They lived in the region along the silver route, including Zacatecas and Guanajuato in Central Mexico, that the Spaniards wanted to control to exploit the mines.[6] After the founding of San Luis de la Paz, the Chichimecs were pushed into the area now known as La Misión. They became sedentary, working in haciendas and mines. The Otomi were agriculturalists living in the valleys of Central Mexico when the Spaniards arrived in 1519. Those who had taken refuge from the Aztecs in Tlaxcala were in charge of defending the frontiers of that small state. They were fierce warriors and attacked Cortés, who defeated them. Later they allied themselves with Cortés against the Aztec king Montezuma. They became conquerors themselves and founded towns such as Querétaro, now a state capital, and subjugated the Chichimecs.

A truce between the Chichimecs, previously enemies of the Spaniards, and the Spaniards and Otomi, by now their converted allies, was agreed to on the date of the founding of the town, August 25, 1552. Coincidently, August 25 is also the celebration date of Saint Louis. San Luis de la Paz is an appropriate choice for the name and the patron saint of this town, since Louis, the French king, was both a crusader and a loving peacemaker. Also, conveniently, it is no doubt relevant that the viceroy at the time was called Luis de Velasco.[7] The term "of peace" (de la Paz) in the name of the town is supposed to celebrate the truce between the two indigenous groups, the Chichimecs and the Otomi.

Some individuals in the communities of Cruz del Palmar and San Luis de la Paz view their fiestas as a contemporary manifestation of the alliance between the Otomis and the Chichimecs following the Chichimec wars, after which the Chichimecs, like the Otomi before them, converted to Catholicism. Thus, these two patron saint fiestas are of symbolic as well as historical importance. Individuals in each of the communities make a pilgrimage to the fiesta of the other and greet one another in an elaborate encounter. This is a very deep relationship that links distant communities, distinct geographically, culturally, socially, and linguistically, that nonetheless feel an ethnic affinity. Such ritual linkages between communities probably exist elsewhere in Mexico and Latin America, but they are rarely reported on in published studies.

The special relationship between Cruz del Palmar and San Luis de la Paz, and particularly the joint celebration of their two patron saint fiestas, is expressed by their sharing their respective saints, who are honored in both places and are brought together at both fiestas, one transported from Cruz del Palmar to San Luis de la Paz and the other transported from San Luis de la Paz to Cruz del Palmar. This custom was explained as follows: "We are united in this devotion. It is our tradition and our custom" (*Estamos unidos en esta devoción. Es nuestra tradición y nuestra costumbre*).

While Cruz del Palmar and San Luis de la Paz are today mestizo communities, many residents consider themselves to be indigenous descendants, and there is a strong indigenous component to the fiestas, and especially to the linking of the two. For this reason we prefer the term Indo-Hispanic to the controversial "mestizo."[8] A few older individuals in Cruz del Palmar speak Otomi, and Otomi cultural practices continue to exist. People remember the times when Otomi was still spoken, and say that the language of the fiesta was Otomi. A ritual leader now in his late fifties told us, "Father spoke to the saints in Otomi" (*Papá les hablaba a los santos en otomi*). In the words of a nephew of a recently deceased man who when younger was a fiesta ritual leader in Cruz del Palmar,

Otomi is very sweet. Well one or another person learned it. But since now there is no one to speak with it is becoming lost. . . . In those days they held the copal burner which they bring with embers, very sweet. With much respect in everything they say, they ask God to help everyone, so that he bless everyone so that they don't miss their daily bread, so that they don't miss some change that is what those who spoke Otomi said. But very sweet, with much tenderness in what they said to God. And now (all in Spanish) it is drier, a little drier but in Otomi no, like everything sweeter.

*Es muy dulce el otomi. Pos una que otra aprendió. Pero como ya no hay con quíen platicar se va olvidando. . . . En aquellos tiempos agarraban el somador ese que traen con las brasitas, muy dulce. Con mucha estimación todo lo que hablan, le piden a Dios que socorra a todos, que bendizca a todos que no les falte el pan de cada día, que no les falten unos cantavitos los que hablaban en otomi. Pero muy dulce, con much cariño que se le habla a Dios. Sí y como que es más seco, un poquito más seco y el otomi no, como que es más dulce todo.*

Even today some ritual specialists, when performing ritual cleansings (limpias), are said to whisper words in Otomi. And this is greatly appreciated.

Chichimec is still spoken in La Misión, though some individuals who consider themselves Chichimec do not speak the language. There is a bilingual education program in schools where children learn to sing the Mexican national anthem in Chichimec. Because of the close ties between Cruz del Palmar and La Misión, there is interest in each other's language. An older woman from La Misión, now deceased, remembered walking with people from Cruz del Palmar. People from each community would ask the other as they walked the names of plants and other things in their respective language. This is a poignant illustration of the respect for each other's language these people felt and still feel, despite the endangered state of both languages.

The Spanish used by the people who participate in the popular religion and fiestas of this region is a local variant of rural Spanish. This dialect differs from standard Spanish mainly in preserving archaisms from the sixteenth century. Its intonation is a bit particular, though not too different from the general intonation of the region, perhaps in a higher tone. Examples of archaisms are *ahoy*, "today" (*hoy* in standard Spanish), *asina*, "this way" (*así* in standard Spanish), *mesmo*, "same" (*mismo* in standard Spanish), *nadien*, "nobody" (*nadie* in standard Spanish), *semos*, "we are" (*somos* in standard Spanish), *vide*, "I saw" (*vi* in standard Spanish), *vido*, "he saw" (*vio* in standard Spanish).

With regard to grammar, *e* is used instead of *i* in the first person plural of some verbs: *pidemos*, "we ask for" (*pedimos* in standard Spanish), *salemos*, "we go out" (*salimos* in standard Spanish), *venemos*, "we come" (*venimos* in standard Spanish). The word *imagen*, feminine in standard Spanish, is masculine in this variety of Spanish. A particular use of the preposition *por* is found in the expression *por tierra*, as in "*antes veníamos por tierra*," which means "we used to walk." The typical diminutive in this region is –*illo*.

Many words or their pronunciations are particular to the Central Mexican patron saint fiesta. In fact, they are not known by individuals who do not participate in these fiestas because they are not familiar with the particular objects or activities they refer to. The resin burner, so important in patron saint fiesta ritual, is called *sahumador* or *sahumerio* in standard Spanish but *somador* in the popular Spanish of this region. Two examples are *ramillete*, which in standard Spanish means little branch or bunch and we translate as altarpiece, and *crucero*, which does not exist in standard Spanish and we translate as adorned panel (see chapter two and the glossary at the end of the book).[9]

The texts of songs and speeches and the quotations from actual speech belong to a range of linguistic registers and styles, from familiar and everyday to formal and poetic. A Spanish speaker might think the speakers are making mistakes in Spanish, but this is not the case. These words, phrases, and expressions are the voices of the people who participate in patron saint fiestas in Central Mexico. The English translation of words and phrases associated with patron saint fiestas presents a challenge because exact equivalents do not exist in English. It was necessary to invent words and phrases that explain or describe the object or its function.

## CALENDAR

Patron saint festival events unfold in both Cruz del Palmar and San Luis de la Paz according to a daily calendar. While there are changes and variations from year to year, the basic structure detailed here shows the ebb and flow and the rhythm of the fiestas. Further description, explanation, and interpretation of these events are provided in the following chapters.

### Cruz del Palmar

**November:** People from the surrounding villages come to Cruz del Palmar to pay homage (*novenas*) to Holy Burial (Santo Entierro).

**November 27:** A ritual request for permission to hold the fiesta is made by the fiesta leader (mayordomo), the official overseeing the preparations for and the conduct of the entire fiesta. This is done in the form of a procession through the town.

**November 28–December 31:** Preparations for the fiesta continue. Money is collected, costumes are made or purchased, dance participants and musical groups are selected, and dance rehearsals commence.

**December 28:** The plant called desert spoon (cucharilla) is gathered. It is used to decorate the adorned panels (cruceros) that are erected in front of the church and the calvaries.

**December 30:** Two simultaneous all-night vigils are held in Cruz del Palmar, the vigil of the flower (*velación de la flor*) and the vigil of the desert spoon (*velación de la cucharilla*).

**December 31:** Participants walk in a procession through Cruz del Palmar to the encounter (*encuentro*) with the visitors from San Luis de La Paz. The adorned panels are placed in front of the calvary and the parish church.

**January 1:** Activities on the day of the patron saint, Holy Burial (Santo Entierro), include a high mass in the parish church atrium at which the priest officiates and a dance drama, the dance of the French and the Apaches (*danza de los franceses y los apaches*), in the square in front of the church. There are also fireworks, the burning of wooden castles and bulls (*quema de castillos y toritos*), and a public dance at night with well-known bands from the United States and Mexico.

**January 2–4:** A rodeo (*jaripeo*) is held, with games, a fair, dances, and the greased pole (*palo encebado*).

**January 5:** The promenade of the cow (*paseo de la vaca*) takes place in the street, and the cow is slaughtered in the morning. In the early afternoon there might be a farewell ceremony for the people of San Luis.

**January 5–6:** A ceremony is held to publicly change or reaffirm the fiesta officials (*cambio de cargos*), with, in the evening, a ritual gathering of breads and blessing of new fiesta officials.

**January 7:** On the final day of the fiesta various activities are scheduled, including a mock battle (*combate*) and a final procession.

## San Luis de la Paz

**August 11–24:** Preparations are made for the fiesta, money is collected, costumes are made, and ritual sites are arranged for.

**August 21:** A ritual request for permission to hold the fiesta is made by the fiesta leader and the official in charge of the dance. This takes place in the chapel of San Luisito.

**August 22:** Desert spoon (cucharilla) is gathered in the morning. A procession takes place where flowers are collected; participants assemble in a house in La Misión with an altar that has been used for the fiesta for about a century. A vigil (velación) takes place at night.

**August 23:** The visitors from Cruz del Palmar arrive, and a vigil is held in the chapel of San Ignacio. Simultaneously, another vigil is held in La Misión, in the same house as the gathering of August 22. It is called the vigil of San Luis (*velación del señor San Luisito*) or the vigil of the adorned panel (*velación del chimal* [called crucero in Cruz del Palmar]), because the participants begin to construct the adorned panel during this vigil.

**August 24:** Participants walk in a procession from a house in La Misión to San Ignacio, with an encounter with visitors from Cruz del Palmar. All process to the church of San Luisito, where other people from San Luis de la Paz join them. Later, people from La Misión return to La Misión and have a ritual meal (*reliquia*) with the guests. The procession with dancers and the adorned panel goes to San Luisito, where the adorned panel is erected.

**August 25:** Activities on August 25, the day of the patron saint, Saint Louis, include masses in San Luisito and the parish church and many secular activities in the streets—music, sports, and the vending in street stands of food, clothing, and utensils. There are many dance groups, including those that come from different neighborhoods and surrounding communities. They take turns dancing in the small square (*placita*) in front of San Luisito and elsewhere, including the streets.

**August 26:** Slaves or devotees (*esclavos, devotos*) of Holy Burial carry the shrines of their saint from the church of San Luisito to the home of the first fiesta leader of the board (*mesa*) of Holy Burial, who presides over the group of slaves. A vigil takes place at night in his home.

**August 27:** A ritual meal is held, attended by the saints' slaves.

**August 28–September 11:** Saints and visitors visit various houses (*posadas*).

**September 12:** People visit each other and the saints.

Additionally, on December 28, an all-night vigil is held for Holy Burial, in preparation for the fiesta of Cruz del Palmar.

From this calendar it can be seen that in both Cruz del Palmar and San Luis de la Paz, recurring activities are basic components of the two patron saint fiestas and structure them. This calendar provides as well an overview that is relevant to the many patron saint fiestas of the region that have similar structures.

These fiestas are not one-day occasions but affairs lasting several days and nights, during which long sequences of multiple, related events occur that have been prepared for during the entire year. In addition, the fiestas are part of a complex of celebrations, encounters, and religious events in Central Mexico and beyond and are a reflection of the popular Catholicism of the area. This highly religious area provides a set of resources, people, symbolic elements, beliefs, and forms of enactment that reappear in different ways in different fiestas. Each village and town and each year has a different combination, a different structuring, and a different organization of the acts and events described here. Some activities are obligatory in a particular community and do not occur in another. Some occur in a particular year and not in others. Sometimes there are giant puppets (*mojigangas*), sometimes there are not; sometimes there is a dance with a body mask or puppet bull (*baile de los toritos*), sometimes there is not; sometimes there are plumed dancers (*danza de pluma, concheros*), sometimes there are not[10]; sometimes a cow is slaughtered, sometimes it is not; sometimes there is a ceremony when fiesta officials are replaced (cambio de cargos), sometimes there is not; sometimes the fiesta ends in a mock battle (combate), sometimes it does not; sometimes a cavalry (*caballería*) attends an outdoor mass, sometimes it does not; sometimes mariachis take part in processions or play at an outdoor mass, sometimes they do not. All of this depends on tradition and the availability of funds.

Some of the fiesta events and moments, such as the fiesta day procession and mass, the final day procession and mass, the burning of the little castles and bulls, the French and Apache dance drama, and the public dances, attract the entire community. Other events involve relatively few people. These include the all-night vigils, the promenade of the cow, and the procession and ceremony of the changing of fiesta officials. Whatever the attendance, everyone knows that the fiesta officials are doing their jobs and the saints are being honored properly.

The following chapters describe in detail the activities that take place during each phase of the patron saint fiestas of Cruz del Palmar and San Luis de la Paz, with references to other fiestas in the region. Chapter two, entitled "Fiesta Leaders, Officials, and Saints," presents the social and ritual system at work in honoring the saints. Chapter three, "Vigils, Visits, and Ritual Meals," is devoted to all-night praying and singing, gatherings essential to fiestas, as well as associated ritual visits and meals. Chapter four, "Processions, Encounters, Ceremonies, and Masses," focuses on the many processions and encounters that are part of these fiestas, as well as on related ceremonies and masses. Chapter five, "Dances, Dance Dramas, and Entertainments," deals with the elaborate choreographed performances and other activities that take place as part of the fiestas. Chapter six, "Toward an Understanding of the Fiesta," offers interpretations of the significance of different elements of patron saint fiestas while considering the past and future of these popular culture events, which constitute a cult of the saints.

Patron saint fiestas with activities similar to the ones described here occur along the silver route that the Spaniards created from Mexico City to Santa Fe. In many communities along this route, traces of the Spanish conquest are reflected in such fiesta activities as conquest dances, religious processions, and adoration of saints. Some examples are the Moors and Christians dance dramas (*Danza de Moros y Cristianos*) in Zacatecas and the Matachines dance in indigenous and Hispanic communities in New Mexico.

Our study documents how religious and aesthetic practices found in fiestas were brought from Spain to Mexico and intermingled with indigenous ones to produce an Indo-Hispanic cultural identity (see chapter six). This book is thus about processes of exchange, acceptance, adaptation, and resistance between and among ethnic groups.

Many of the performances we describe, including the singing of ballads, the dances and dance dramas, and the adoration of Catholic saints, are a replay of relations of power and domination between Spain and the indigenous New World. Thus, patron saint fiestas are the scene of the surging out of an indigenous past, more or less overtly or consciously, in language, music, dance, costume, practices, beliefs, and performances.

We have made a point of focusing on the mingling, intersections, and layerings of forms, linguistic, musical, gestural, poetic, and olfactory, because they are the elements that create thickness and depth and impart a special atmosphere, both sacred and profane, to the fiesta. Through our participation we experienced for ourselves the transformation of time in fiestas, from ordinary work and leisure periods to ritual celebration day and night.

Several themes recur in this book as we present the different activities of the patron saint fiestas. These themes include the importance of the Catholic faith, the deep love and respect for the saint, the importance of the ancestors who first adopted the Catholic religion, the co-presence of indigenous and Hispanic elements, the constant concern about mortality, and the necessity of enduring the sacrifice that the patron saint fiesta entails. Indeed, in the words of Enrique Lomadrid, what is negotiated in the patron saint fiestas is "an ancient dialogue across cultures about history, heritage, and identity."[11]

FIGURE I.I
*Location of Cruz del Palmar, San Luis de la Paz, and La Misión de los Chichimecas.*
*Drawing by Fernando Botas.*

FIGURE I.2
*Landscape of Cruz del Palmar. Photograph by Yolanda Lastra.*

FIGURE I.3
*Landscape near La Misión neighborhood of San Luis de la Paz.*
*Photograph by Yolanda Lastra.*

FIGURE I.4
*Parish church of Cruz del Palmar with adorned panels* (cruceros).
*Photograph by Yolanda Lastra.*

FIGURE I.5
*Church of San Luisito in San Luis de la Paz. Photograph by Yolanda Lastra.*

# TWO

# FIESTA LEADERS, OFFICIALS, AND SAINTS

## (*Mayordomos, cargueros, y santos*)

### FIESTA LEADERS AND OFFICIALS

For a patron saint fiesta to occur, an extraordinarily complex organization must be put in place. Many individuals with specific abilities and talents must be mobilized to carry out specific tasks. A network of social and economic ties must be activated, and adequate funding must be found. Central to this organization are the individuals who take on civil-religious roles called *cargos*. *Cargos* literally means burdens, and both metaphorically and in practice the term refers to roles or duties. The individuals who hold these roles are the fiesta leaders (*mayordomos*) and officials (*cargueros*) (the origins of this system are discussed in chapter six). Being a fiesta leader or official is a significant and respected role in the community. The duties of leaders imply knowledge of what needs to be done and a commitment of finances and time. These duties are transmitted in hereditary fashion from generation to generation in some places. In others, new individuals are named each year.

Patron saint fiestas require a large investment of money as well as effort. Although some of the funds might come from the church and the government, most consist of contributions from families, from people who live in the community and their relatives who no longer live there but come for the fiesta from other places—Mexican cities, including the capital, Mexico City, and the "other side" (*el otro lado*), the north (*el norte*), or the United States. Individuals and groups in the community, in other parts of Mexico, and in the United States work together to bring about the fiesta. Some officials told us they preferred not to take money from the government so as to preserve their independence and have the fiesta the way they want it.

The complex organization of a patron saint fiesta presupposes networks, ties, financial means, commitment, and willingness to help, get involved, and work. Although the fiesta leaders and the officials are in charge of everything, their wives and children contribute in important ways to the activities. In fact, whole families—brothers and sisters, husbands and wives, and children—all work together. Fiesta leaders and officials also draw on ritual kin, such as godparents (*compadres*), as well as family members. Women prepare food and make costumes, play instruments, sing, dance, and care for the saints. Some women are actively involved in the fiesta ritual. In some communities, no procession is complete without a female ritual leader (*tenancha*) walking at the head of the procession carrying a red flag (*la pasión*) and ringing a small bell. This paraphernalia—the flag and the bell—is sometimes called *la rosa*. It is noteworthy that women, including female ritual leaders, play important roles in patron saint fiestas.

The fiesta leaders (mayordomos) are businessmen, entrepreneurs, managers, and organizers. They oversee the conduct of the fiesta and work with officials to make sure the various activities of the fiesta are organized and executed properly. These activities include gathering various plants, purchasing or otherwise obtaining food, flowers, stick rockets (*cohetes*), and fireworks, making costumes, overseeing the rehearsals of dancers and musicians, decorating the town and the church, and, most important, taking care of the saints. The build-up to the fiesta and the associated preparations proceed to an intimate and intense crescendo, with everyone working, collaborating, and contributing.

The role of the fiesta leaders is pragmatic, materialistic, and efficient, as well as spiritual and sacred. They lead the performance of the Four Winds (*Cuatro Vientos*) ceremony, and they purify people and objects in cleansing ceremonies (limpias). In many communities they are in charge of asking permission from God, the saint, and the departed souls (*ánimas*) to hold the fiesta. The departed souls are deceased community members (an example of a permission text is given in appendix C2). These permission ceremonies can occur in various places, such as a calvary or a cemetery. The fiesta leaders are intercessors between the village or town and the patron saints; some of them are recognized as being endowed with special powers and abilities and are recognized as curers and healers. In addition, they participate in helping to build objects, lead processions, and play instruments and sing, and they host meals in their houses. Patron saint fiesta leaders and other officials are also eloquent orators. They make speeches during gatherings, welcoming or bidding farewell to visitors and counseling officials (see examples in the various appendices). They have a historical perspective on the traditions, the history, and the significance of the activities of the patron saint fiesta. In their speeches they explain to others the meaning and importance of various aspects of the fiesta.

The officials (cargueros) who work with the fiesta leader have specific duties connected to their role or to the activity or event for which they are responsible. They have to find the personnel, the objects, and the money to bring their task to fruition. Often they call on itinerant specialists, including musicians, who are known in the region and who travel to or are invited from place to place to officiate at an all-night vigil, play music, participate in a dance in honor of the saint, or otherwise perform a ritual role. While the carguero system is widespread, local differences and variations exist, in both terminology and practice.[1] A description of the carguero organizations in Cruz del Palmar and San Luis de la Paz illustrates the multifaceted functions and activities of the patron saint fiesta leaders and officials.

## SAINTS

Saints are particularly important to practitioners of popular religion in this region. They are a significant part of the religiosity and are omnipresent in people's lives. The adoration of the saints is both personal and collective. Related to saints and treated like them are manifestations of Christ (such as the Holy Burial, Santo Entierro, the patron saint of Cruz del Palmar), the Virgin Mary, the cross, and the Virgin of Guadalupe.[2] Spaniards brought the saints and other elements of the Catholic religion, and their introduction into this region is related to the history of the Dominican, Franciscan, and Jesuit presence, and more generally to the history of conquest and conversion. The Spanish missionaries built many churches and chapels, often with the help of the Indians. Churches were often fortified to provide protection against the enemy Indians, but they were also places of learning. The friars taught religion, music, and crafts. Their main goal, however, was to convert the Indians to Catholicism. They performed masses, baptisms, burials, and religious plays. Through the work of the friars, indigenous and Hispanic traditions were joined together, as can be observed today in the patron saint fiesta.[3]

Indigenous people were often permitted to choose their own saints, and they chose them according to similarities with their deities. The dates of former agricultural rituals often coincide with dates of the celebration of a saint.[4] Saints are central components in patron saint fiestas; in fact, the fiestas are essentially a cult of the saints. The beliefs and practices associated with the saints today are a mixture of Mesoamerican indigenous beliefs and practices, in particular Aztec and Otomi, and Spanish ones.

As in other parts of Mexico, representations of the saints in the form of images, statues, drawings, and paintings are ubiquitous.[5] Some take the form of small, doll-like portable statues (*demanditas* or *santitos*), which are kept in small glass shrines and displayed on altars in churches, chapels, and private homes during vigils and visits. These statues and crosses are treasured by the people and have been in their church for many generations; they are often antique objects of great value and beauty. Unfortunately, they are also objects of theft, and some have ended up in the hands of antique dealers.

Saints are associated with individuals and social groups of various kinds, including villages and towns. These communities may be named after a saint. Saints are honored and adored in many ways. During the fiesta days set aside specifically for them, various activities are organized. As one ritual leader told us, "The fiesta is to please the saint" (*La fiesta es para agradecer al santo*). The activities vary according to region. In the region around Cruz del Palmar and San Luis de la Paz, during the fiestas saints are honored by visitors, who, nine days before the fiesta, come to the parish church to visit the saint, recite prayers, and bring flowers for him (*novenario*) The priest of the parish church presides at a mass on the saint's day in honor of the saint and often closes the fiesta with a mass for him. People hold all-night vigils (*velaciones*) for the saints during which they pray and sing. Elaborate dances and dance dramas are performed in honor of the saints. Saints are transported, displayed, and carried lovingly during processions and encounters. They travel for visits (*posadas*) with different families, and ritual meals (*reliquias*) take place in their honor. Mariachi or brass bands play in front of the church and other sacred spaces on the saint's day. The bands are hired to play for the saint in early morning (*mañanitas*). Sometimes they play in the afternoon (*tardecitas*) or evening (*nochecitas*).

A set of ritual objects is an intrinsic part of the cult of the saints and particular to this region. People who do not participate in patron saint fiestas in this region do not know these objects, their names, or the special vocabulary associated with them. Adorned panels (called *cruceros* in Cruz del Palmar and *chimales* in San Luis) are heavy rectangular structures, approximately thirty feet long and five feet wide. As many as sixteen men may be needed to carry them. Typically an adorned panel has one side decorated with a cross or other pattern and the other side has two extensions that are used as handles to transport it during processions and then to erect it vertically against or in front of a church or a calvary. The frame of the adorned panel is made of pine or other strong wood and holds a bed (*cama*) made with transverse lattices of reed (carrizo). The frame and the transverse lattices are saved for use from year to year.

A group of men with special knowledge and skill reconstruct the adorned panels each year. The first task is to undress (*desvestir*) the panel, that is, to prepare the lattices, taking out broken or rotten pieces and the decorations from the previous year. Then they shorten the leaves of the desert spoon, cucharilla, and carefully peel away the thorns. Once the thorns are cut out the desert spoon becomes an artichoke-leaf-like bulb. When part of the leaf is detached from the bulb, it looks like a little spoon of a whitish mother-of-pearl color.[6] The men then insert these pieces into the reed lattices to create designs and patterns, with different ones on each adorned panel. This process is called "weaving the adorned panel" (*tejer el crucero*) and requires skill and precision. Now the panel is again dressed (*vestido*). In addition, offerings such as colorful breads or cans of beer are also attached to the panel. The finished product is an elaborate work of art that looks to some like a huge stretcher and to others like a huge shield, but it is used neither to carry nor to protect. The word *crucero* might seem to be derived from the word *cruz* (cross), but this object is not used in any way like a Catholic cross. Some say that the adorned panel "is an offering to the dead, an homage that is paid to the 'conquerer souls,' that is, the tutelary dead who in ancient times 'lost their lives in order to gain souls for the Christian faith'" (*es una ofrenda a los muertos, un homenaje que se hace a las 'ánimas conquistadoras,' es decir, los muertos tutelares que antiguamente 'perdieron su vida para ganar almas a la fe cristiana'*).[7]

Another object, an altarpiece called a ramillete ("little branch or bunch"), recalls in form the monstrance used in the official Catholic Church. Like the adorned panel, it must be made out of desert spoon (cucharilla), but it also requires fennel and carnations inserted onto and woven into a preexisting round wooden frame, from a previous year's altarpiece that, again like the adorned panel, has been undressed (desvestido) and for this year's fiesta needs to be dressed (vestido) again. This happens during an all-night vigil.

The altarpiece is also a work of art. It is a circular flower-like construction with four points. The circular part is connected to a vertical stand twenty centimeters high and combines four colors: the light brown of its wooden frame, the green of the fennel, the red of a carnation, and the whitish mother-of-pearl color of the desert spoon. Several men work for two to three hours cutting, weaving, inserting, and sewing the various elements together. When the altarpiece is ready, it is used to ritually cleanse participants in the vigil. With it the ritual leader performs the ceremony of the Four Winds (Cuatro Vientos). The altarpiece is also carried during the procession along with the saints and ends up in the church, not on the altar but on the steps in front of the altar. People say that the four points of the altarpiece correspond to the four winds and the four cardinal directions, as well as to the four points of the cross and the four Evangelists, Matthew, Mark, Luke, and John.

The saint receives offers of flowers, candles, and resin (*copal*). Resin in the form of small white translucent crystals, bought in markets, is used instead of incense to perfume the saint and to cleanse participants in various rituals. It burns in a resin burner (*sahumerio,* locally called *somerio*), a clay vessel that has a leg and can stand by itself or be held while the resin is burning and releasing its very distinctive scented smoke. It is the equivalent of the Catholic Church's incense burner, but with a very different smell. The smoke in the resin burner has ritual value. In the words of the people involved, "Resin is for perfuming the saints, candles are for lighting the saint, to accompany him. He is offered his resin, his little flowers, his candles" (*El copal es para somar los santitos, las velas son para alumbrar el santito, para acompañarlo. Se le ofrece su copal, sus florecitas, sus ceras*). People call the smoke of the copal "the word" (*la palabra*).

During vigils and processions, a set of four items must be present: a red flag (la pasión), a little bell (campanita), a candle (vela), and resin (copal). All the activities of the fiesta and the objects described here are created or purchased for it and are designed to honor the saints.

Two striking practices that do not exist in traditional Catholicism take place at various moments of the patron saint fiesta: ritual cleansing (limpia) and the Four Winds (Cuatro Vientos) ceremony. On the patron saint's day, people arriving at a ritual event, such as a vigil, or before entering a church or chapel, carry offerings of flowers or candles, which they hand to the ritual leader and kneel in front of him while he stands. The ritual leader takes these objects and makes the sign of the cross with them over the kneeling person, an action they believe purifies the recipient of the blessing. He softly says a prayer, either in Spanish or in an indigenous language. This event is called a cleansing. The fiesta leader can also perform a cleansing with the resin burner. He then makes the sign of the cross with it in space. This action is intended to cleanse the space, to rid the space and the people of evil. Such cleansings take place during vigils, encounters, and other significant moments of patron saint fiestas.

While cleansings are performed for single individuals, the Four Winds ceremony is carried out by a group of people under the direction of a ritual leader, in front of a church, saint, cross, or altar, and as part of a vigil or procession. The people, who are standing, first face the church, the saint, the cross, or the altar, then turn their backs to it, then turn their bodies to the left and then to the right. In each position the ritual leader, often kneeling, makes the sign of the cross with his smoking resin burner. This ceremony, like the cleansing, is intended to rid the persons and place of bad spirits or evil thoughts or intentions that might exist, as well as to perfume the saint. It is also an invocation of the forces of nature as it involves all the elements of nature, including Earth. It is intended to induce well-being and harmony.[8]

Early on in the history of Mexican patron saint fiestas a social, affective, and material texture developed around the image of the saint.[9] This is still the case today. People participating in the adoration of their patron saint probably know the particular attributes associated with the saint. But they never invoke hagiographic information as part of the events of the fiesta. People adore the saints because they believe in their power to prevent disease, help curing, alleviate pains, prevent envy and jealousy, ward off tragedy, and take care of departed souls of the ancestors (ánimas). Individuals have specific requests of the saints and in hopes of successfully getting them they make special promises (*mandas*) to the saints, in the form of specific actions or behaviors, such as praying, giving money for the fiesta, walking on their knees as penitents in a procession, or performing in dances. When we ask people what the saint means for them, they explain: "one asks the saint that he provide life and health" (*se le pide al santo que preste vida y salud*), "that he accompany you" (*que te acompañe*), "that he open doors for you" (*que te abra las puertas*), "that he help you" (*que te ayude*), and "that he bring you luck" (*que te traiga suerte*).

People feel a personal intimacy with the saint. They refer to him as el Santito, San Luisito, or Santo Entierrito, using the diminutive of affection, endearment, and respect. This verbal practice, derived from the indigenous languages Nahuatl and Otomi, is honorific and signifies respect. And there is definitely respect for as well as deference to the saint. In preparation for the fiesta, the statue of the saint is washed and provided with new clothes. During processions and encounters saints are kissed in their shrines. Men and women cross themselves in front of them, address them directly, and explain their emotional, psychological, and physical concerns. Through singing and praying, making offerings and promises, people enter into a special relationship with the saint. People who are adepts of the cult of the saints share a special type of subjectivity shaped by their beliefs, spirituality, and ritual knowledge and practices. The devotion displayed by people of all ages, men and women, is striking. People who may not attend Catholic Church services regularly honor their saint during his patron saint fiesta.

## FIESTA LEADERS, OFFICIALS, AND SAINTS IN CRUZ DEL PALMAR

The fiesta of Holy Burial (Santo Entierro) in Cruz del Palmar is an elaborate multiday celebration requiring many organizers and many tasks. At the head of this organization is the fiesta leader (mayordomo), responsible for and orchestrating all activities. He participates in two ceremonies that emphasize the importance of his role. On November 27, he asks permission of the saint and the departed souls to hold the fiesta, and on January 5 and 6 he presents the new officials (cargueros) to the community during the changing of duties (cambio de cargos), a ceremony during which they pay allegiance to both the saint and the village. The request for permission and the changing of duties announce the fiesta and its officials to the community and ensure continuity from year to year. One of the fiesta leader's duties is to plan and host the stay of the visitors from San Luis de la Paz who come to Cruz del Palmar to participate in the fiesta of Holy Burial from late December until early January. He has to organize the trip of people from Cruz del Palmar who go to San Luis de la Paz in late August to participate in the fiesta of Saint Louis. He stays there for the various vigils (velaciones), ritual meals (reliquias), and visits (posadas).

One or several officials undertake specific duties. One set of officials is in charge of building the adorned panels (cruceros) that will be erected in front of the church. Officials and assistants must gather materials needed for making adorned panels. On December 28 they gather the desert spoon (cucharilla), sometimes traveling great distances to do so.

Four adorned panels are built each year. Each of the adorned panels is built outside the house of the official in charge of building it. At precise times during the fiesta a group of men erects one of the panels in front of the calvary on the hill and three others in the atrium of the parish church. The adorned panels in the atrium are related to the three dances of the rattles (sonajas) performed by groups of young children throughout the fiesta in front of them. The panels and the dance groups are centrally and intimately related to the fiesta as a whole. The officials responsible for each dance group are also responsible for the respective adorned panel. The adorned panel erected in front of the calvary on the hill is not associated with a dance group.

The official responsible for the dance of the French and the Apaches that takes place outside the atrium of the parish church oversees the choreography, music, costumes, and rehearsals and provides meals to the dancers and the musicians, as does the official of the dances of the rattles. Still another official is responsible for contacting and inviting the "crazies" (locos). The crazies are a group of individuals dressed in outrageous outfits who dance to the sounds of contemporary Latin music blasting from a sound system at various moments of the fiesta. Another official invites the giant puppets (mojigangas), who participate in processions or perform dances.

Other officials, with help from assistants, take charge of several activities. Some, in collaboration with the local priest, must prepare for the huge mass that takes place outside in the atrium of the parish church on the main day of the fiesta. They see to it that a stage is erected and decorated in front of the church. Others select and contact musical groups, specialists of stick rockets (cohetes) and fireworks. And still others are responsible for special events, such as the all-night vigils, the many processions, the purchasing of flowers and ritual plants, the taking care of the saints, and the decoration of the town and the church.

The music that needs to be provided is extensive. Officials must find groups of musicians, either from Cruz del Palmar or itinerant groups from the region who go from fiesta to fiesta, and famous groups that come from the United States. Music played by a trio of string instruments is an integral part of all-night vigils; brass bands accompany processions and perform in the kiosk in the central plaza; mariachi bands play at masses; and huge bands play at all-night public dances. Of course, the bell ringer of the parish church is very active, dramatically punctuating various moments of the fiesta.

The patron saint of Cruz del Palmar, Holy Burial, is actually a manifestation of Christ, associated in the official Catholic Church with Good Friday, the day of the death of Christ, but whose official day as the patron saint of Cruz del Palmar is January 1. Of the various ways Santo Entierro is translated into English, including "Entombed Christ" and "Reclining Christ," we have selected Holy Burial as the most appropriate because of the translation of Santo as Holy.

Representations of Holy Burial are found in several places in Cruz del Palmar. Inside the parish church he lies dramatically in a large glass shrine on the right side of the altar. This is a recent acquisition. The crucifix above the altar, which has been in the parish church much longer, is also Holy Burial, even though he is not lying down. It is an articulated statue that can be laid down or nailed to the cross. Holy Burial also exists as a small shrine (demandita) that can travel and be taken to vigils, except when the priest objects to it. Some people own small shrines of Holy Burial that they place on their home altars. Some also own a shrine of Saint Louis, because of the ritual linkage with San Luis de la Paz. In Cruz del Palmar, Holy Burial is revered along with other saints, in particular the medical saints (santos médicos) Cosmé and Damian, and the Virgin of Guadalupe, all of whom are found in the parish church. As the calendar in chapter one shows, Holy Burial is honored during vigils, masses, processions, dances, and other activities to be described in the following chapters.

## FIESTA LEADERS, OFFICIALS, AND
## SAINTS IN SAN LUIS DE LA PAZ

In San Luis de la Paz two fiesta leaders (mayordomos) organize every aspect and event of the fiesta and must coordinate the activities of San Luis de la Paz and those of nearby La Misión. The first fiesta leader (mayordomo primero) is responsible for what needs to happen in the city of San Luis de la Paz and the second fiesta leader (mayordomo segundo) is responsible for La Misión. These two fiesta leaders collaborate with officials (here not called cargueros) whose positions are hereditary. Distinct from Cruz del Palmar, there is not a transfer-of-duties ceremony every year in San Luis de la Paz. In general, the fiesta leader and officials in San Luis de la Paz have the same duties as those of Cruz del Palmar, and in fact of any fiesta leader in the region — to build the adorned panels (here called *chimal*) and make sure that all other necessary objects (stick rockets, fireworks, flowers, decorations) are obtained or made and all activities (vigils, visits, dances) are carried out. The two fiesta leaders must also host the visitors from Cruz del Palmar in August during the fiesta of Saint Louis and go to Cruz del Palmar for the fiesta of Holy Burial from late December until early January. In addition to the activities organized in La Misión, many neighborhoods of San Luis have officials who train dance groups and lead them to the large procession of August 25.

The patron saint of San Luis de la Paz, including La Misión, is San Luis, or Saint Louis, the French medieval king, the king of the crusades in the Holy Land and also the king of kindness and peace. As in most places whose patron saint is Saint Louis, his day is August 25, and August 25 is the day of the fiesta in San Luis de la Paz.

Saint Louis is honored in two churches in San Luis de la Paz. One is the large parish church in the center of town, on the square (jardín), and the other is the intimate chapel of San Luisito, in front of a small square also in the center of town. A vigil is held in the chapel of the neighborhood of San Ignacio, next to la Misión, where the encounter between the people of Cruz del Palmar and San Luis de la Paz takes place. Just as Holy Burial is honored on home altars, in churches, at vigils and dances, and in processions in Cruz del Palmar, Saint Louis is honored on home altars, in churches, at vigils and dances, and in processions in San Luis de la Paz and La Misión.

A striking and elaborate practice in San Luis de la Paz is the existence of an active confraternity called the board of slaves (*mesa de esclavos*), dedicated to the devotion of Holy Burial, the patron saint of Cruz del Palmar. These slaves commit themselves to a set of ritual activities that include visits to Holy

Burial in Cruz del Palmar on the day of his fiesta. When slaves go to Cruz del Palmar to the fiesta to venerate Holy Burial, they are supposed to bring an offering and greet their sponsoring godfather (*padrino*) or godmother (*madrina*) in Cruz del Palmar. When people from Cruz del Palmar go to the fiesta of Saint Louis in San Luis de la Paz, they are obligated to participate in the ritual activities of the board. New members are introduced to the board when someone asks to be inducted before a ritual meal (reliquia). The induction ceremony is called a coronation (*coronación*), and the new inductees are called the crowned ones (*coronados*). The first fiesta leader (mayordomo) explains to the new members their obligations. These are for life. New slaves choose their godfathers, and if the godfathers accept, an induction ceremony takes place. The inductee kneels before the altar with a candle in his or her hand. Their godfathers stand behind them and put their hand on the shoulder of the new member. They arrange the red banner of the female ritual leader (tenancha) in such a way that a little piece of it touches the new slave. Musicians play the guitar, banjo, and armadillo shell (concha), and the female ritual leader rings her little bell. The godchild and the godfather say the Lord's Prayer. The fiesta leader receives the candle and puts it on the altar.

Slaves engage in a series of verbal and nonverbal ritual acts. They call each other godfather or godmother and greet each other ritually by starting to embrace from a distance and then moving closer and touching each other and kissing each other's hand. In the case of a young woman and an old man, he kisses her hand first and then she kisses his. When a godson or goddaughter greets his or her godfather or godmother the godchild kneels in front of the godparent and kisses the godparent's hand, then is blessed in turn by the godparent. In leave-taking the same ritual acts are performed.

Slaves take part in ritual meals (reliquias) during which they are served special food and drink, including bread and atole. They host visits (posadas) during which the saint stays in their house and they pray for him, offering him flowers, perfuming him with resin (copal), and welcoming visitors who come to pay their respect to the saint. Visitors are supposed to give alms, which are later brought to the priest of the parish church of Cruz del Palmar.

In presenting fiesta leaders, officials, and saints, we have introduced the actors, places, spaces, objects, and practices that together play a role in the patron saint fiestas of Cruz del Palmar and San Luis de la Paz. They are the components of emergent structures taking place year after year in each community in honor of the saints and having ritual, symbolic, and social significance. We develop these in subsequent chapters.

**FIGURE 2.1**
*Altar in house in San Luis de la Paz. Photograph by Yolanda Lastra.*

**FIGURE 2.2**
*Figure of Saint Louis in a shrine. Photograph by Yolanda Lastra.*

FIGURE 2.3
*Fiesta officials making an adorned panel* (crucero). *Photograph by Yolanda Lastra.*

FIGURE 2.4
*Desert spoon* (cucharilla). *Photograph by Yolanda Lastra.*

FIGURE 2.5
*Dancers erecting an adorned panel in front of a* calvario *in Cruz del Palmar.*
*Photograph by Yolanda Lastra.*

FIGURE 2.6
*Adorned panel inside the parish church atrium in Cruz del Palmar.*
*Photograph by Yolanda Lastra.*

FIGURE 2.7

*Adorned panel in San Luis de la Paz. Photograph by Yolanda Lastra.*

FIGURE 2.8
*Altarpiece (ramillete). Photograph by Joel Sherzer.*

FIGURE 2.9
*Musicians performing for the saint in front of the parish church in Cruz del Palmar.*
*Photograph by Joel Sherzer.*

FIGURE 2.10
*Fiesta leader performing a ritual cleansing. Photograph by Joel Sherzer.*

FIGURE 2.11
*Fiesta leader blessing an adorned panel. Photograph by Joel Sherzer.*

# THREE

# VIGILS, VISITS, AND RITUAL MEALS

## (*Velaciones, posadas, y reliquias*)

Visitors walking around a neighborhood or a village in the evening after dark in the region of Cruz del Palmar and San Luis de la Paz during a patron saint fiesta are likely to come across a house or a courtyard where people are gathered and are singing, accompanied by various string instruments. They probably will not know or have never heard this type of singing or this type of music, because they have never attended a vigil (velación). These vigils, which are obligatory at patron saint fiestas, are intense moments of performance, togetherness, sociability, and devotion. They usually last all night and are intimate gatherings of people who come to honor one or several saints placed on an altar. The participants, of all ages, from young children to elderly adults, gather in a room in a private house, in the local church, or outside under a protective covering. They sit on chairs, benches, stools, or mats (*petates*) on the cement floor, or simply on the ground. Women bring their small children, who often fall asleep wrapped in their mother's shawl (*rebozos*). Visitors keep coming individually or in groups of persons from a single family, or a group of friends. The people present sing hymns and ballads, both called *alabanzas,* accompanied by musicians. The visitors and the people from the house as well as the musicians receive ritual cleansings (limpias). The ritual leader of the vigil directs the participants in an enactment of the Four Winds (Cuatro Vientos) ceremony. The singing is interrupted by breaks during which food and drink are served and people talk, joke, and smoke cigarettes.

Vigils are part of the preparation for fiestas and occur while men make ritual objects, the adorned panels (cruceros) or altarpieces (ramilletes). Vigils are held during the visits of guests from one or the other of the ritually linked communities of Cruz del Palmar and San Luis de la Paz. In Cruz del Palmar they are also part of the ceremony of the changing of duties, that is, the selection of the next year's fiesta officials. In addition to these moments, in

San Luis de la Paz they are held after the patron saint fiesta (after August 25) during the series of visits in which the saint is taken from house to house.

Vigils have no fixed starting time, and people come and go as they please. Especially in the winter in this region, a striking aspect of vigils is the contrast between hot and cold. It is very cold outside but warm inside. The blessing, singing, eating, drinking, and joking, the beauty of the altar, and the smell of burning resin (copal) provide a warmth, friendliness, and aesthetic quality to the social and religious communion of the event. Burning resin and lit candles and their smoke lend an aura of ritual to the scene. Vigils can occur before, during, and after fiestas, during visits (posadas), and after ritual meals (reliquias).

The activities for the vigil take place in several spaces. In the kitchen of the house women prepare food and drink. In the inner courtyard of or a room in the house, a group of men make an altarpiece or an adorned panel. A room in a house or a courtyard under an awning becomes the center of ritual activities where an altar is erected and where blessing, singing, and talking, as well as joking, take place. On the altar rest the shrines of the saints or a replica of the cross, depending on who or what is being honored. Flower and fruit offerings, candles, Coca-Cola, rubbing alcohol, and resin held in a resin burner (somerio) stand next to the saints. The altar is a busy, complex, religious site, beautiful and bountiful.

The leader of the vigil, a ritual specialist, opens the evening's events with the Four Winds ceremony in front of the altar. Holding the resin burner, he leads the participants, who stand at this moment, in turning successively in the four cardinal directions. This ceremony is performed to please the saint and purify the space. During the evening the leader also performs the cleansing ceremony for the persons who are present or who come in and one by one kneel in front of him with an offering of a candle, flowers, or resin for the saint. The purpose of the vigil is to worship and care for the saint. It is also to keep company (acompañar) the men who are making an adorned panel or an altarpiece.

During much of the vigil, a single musician or, more commonly, a group of three or four musicians play instruments and sing. The leader of the musicians may be the ritual leader of the vigil who performs the Four Winds and cleansing rituals. The musicians play an armadillo shell (concha), a lute-like string instrument, or a guitar, mandolin, or banjo. They are often from the village or town in which the fiesta takes place; they might also have been invited or hired in from elsewhere. During the vigil people sing traditional Catholic hymns and corrido-like ballads, recounting historical moments or events characteristic of this area of Mexico and focusing on their religion. People know the hymns and ballads by heart and sing them with devotion. They have heard and sung them all their lives. Sometimes one of the performers looks at an old weathered book that contains the songs they are singing. These books, not found in churches or religious stores or stands in the area, contain the classic favorite ballads sung over the years during vigils. Ritual leaders treasure these old books that confer an authenticity, literacy, and prestige on the event. Some musicians in the region compose new ballads that they sing when they are invited. These practices reveal the interest of honoring and continuing traditions and at the same time creating new texts on the model of the old ones.

The musicians play in unison, strumming mainly on the downbeats, and perform some instrumental percussion. People sing in unison. Women sing in high voice, men with a tense vocal timbre. The ballads have a strophic structure with refrains. They are in a major key with simple diatonic harmonies. The distinctive timbre of the concha accompaniment is noticeable. Among the ballads we have heard are "With Permission from God the Father" (*Con licencia de Dios Padre*), "The Great Tenochtitlán" (*La gran Tenochtitlán*), "Lord of Villaseca" (*Señor de Villaseca*), "The Musicians Go Two by Two" (*Van los concheros de dos en dos*), "The Year Nineteen Hundred" (*Año de mil nuevecientos*), "The Lord of Esquipula" (*Señor de Esquipula*), and "Star of the East" (*Estrella del Oriente*) (texts in Spanish and English translations appear in appendix B1). Their performance, style, and structure are particular to the context of the vigil. The texts are characterized by a poetic parallelism reminiscent of both indigenous chants and European ballad forms featuring rhymes and repetitions.[1] As is evident from the texts, the songs exhibit a remarkable amount of cultural, historical, and mythical references pertaining to the knowledge and beliefs of the people practicing this popular religion.

"With Permission from God the Father" (*Con licencia de Dios Padre*), a twelve-stanza song, usually opens a vigil. Stanzas two to five summon the prehispanic four winds and link them to the European Christian four Evangelists, Mathew, Mark, Luke, and John. Here is stanza two, relating the first wind to John.

> Let us form the first wind
> let us form the first wind
> to the soul of Saint John
> to the soul of Saint John
> who is in the Gospel.

*Formemos el primer viento*
*formemos el primer viento*
*del ánima de San Juan*
*del ánima de San Juan*
*que en el Evangelio está.*

For each stanza, the verbal forms state that the action of summoning the winds and the evangelists is taking place at the moment of the performance of the song. Stanza nine involves Saint James (Santiago), the patron saint of Spain, who is supposed to have appeared in the sky riding his horse. Always represented as a rider, he is considered to be the messenger of the Four Winds, thus uniting prehispanic indigenous and Catholic beliefs. The text says,

Long live Lord St James
long live Lord St James
because he is the messenger
because he is the messenger
of the Four Winds.

*Que viva Señor Santiago*
*que viva Señor Santiago*
*porque él es el correo*
*porque él es el correo*
*de los Cuatro Vientos.*

The set of parallel repetitions and rhyme schemes that gives this stanza its poetic and rhythmic quality is present in all the other stanzas as well.

The expression "He is God" (*El es Dios*) in stanza seven is frequently heard during speeches, ritual meals, vigils, and visits. According to a legend, the Chichimecs said *El es Dios* when they saw a bright light in the sky that made them stop their battle against the Otomi Indians, who had already been converted to Christianity and were allies of the Spaniards. This utterance expresses the deep religiosity of these people and their full acceptance of God and Christianity. Stanza eight invokes a lonely soul (*el ánima sola*) that, the song says, is in the Cathedral of Mexico City. This lonely soul, according to popular belief, is in purgatory because nobody prays for it and it is not honored by the living. It is believed that a lonely soul needs to have people pray for it, otherwise it might bring evil. In paintings, the soul is depicted as a woman surrounded by flames. In stanza ten, the conqueror souls (*las ánimas conquistadoras*) are the souls of the ancestors who became Christians and converted people to the Catholic faith. They are invoked in the song along with the souls of ritual leaders from the town or the village who have died and who are mentioned by name. Lonely and conqueror souls, nahuals, the weeping woman (*la llorona*), and other such manifestations in Mexican popular culture are invisible beings that affect the living and need to be cared for and pacified. In addition to appearing in hymns sung during vigils, lonely souls and conqueror souls often have stories told about them.

Composed of ten stanzas, "The Great Tenochtitlán" (*La gran Tenochtitlán*), despite its historical anachronisms, recounts the history of the Spanish conquest and the conversion to Christianity of the Indians that took place in Mexico. Stanzas one through eight list several events that occurred during the conquest. Stanza one introduces the theme that nobody saw what happened in the great Tenochtitlán, the capital of the Aztec empire. Notice the proudly used first person plural possessive, "our" (*nuestra*) America.

> When our America
> was conquered
> with all its inhabitants
> no one saw anything
> over there in the great Tenochtitlán.

> *Cuando nuestra América*
> *fue conquistada*
> *de todos los habitantes*
> *ninguno vido nada*
> *allá en la gran en la gran Tenochtitlán.*

Stanza two says that Cortés conquered the Indians through religion. Stanza three imagines an encounter between Cortés and Christopher Columbus, symbolizing together the conquest of the New World and the importance of religion in this endeavor. Stanza four evokes the Aztec king Cuauhtemoc, who fought valiantly against Cortés and was defeated and taken prisoner. Stanza five says that Malinche, Cortés's interpreter and companion, was baptized, and stanza six repeats the theme expressed in stanza one and that also ends the song, namely, that nobody in Tenochititlán saw anything. Stanza seven says that the Chichimec Indians were baptized. Stanzas eight and nine refer to the famous battle of San Grimal. The hill of San Grimal is the legendary place where Chichimecs and Otomis fought and where the Holy Cross appeared, putting an end to the battle in 1531.

This beautiful song, with its recurring, incantatory verse, "Over there in the great Tenochititlán" (*Allá en la gran Tenochititlán*), is striking for its double or ambiguous messages. On the one hand, it praises the Aztec empire, calling its capital the great Tenochititlán. At the same time it praises the conquest and the conversions that were imposed on the Indians and imply that they, the Indians, were and are grateful for this. In addition, three times the song states that the inhabitants of Tenochititlán "saw nothing" (*ninguno vido nada*) (the verb *vido* is a sixteenth-century form of *vio*, "he saw"), which could mean that the Aztecs did not realize the importance of the conquest and the Catholic religion.

It is worth remembering that the people of the region who sing this song during vigils consider themselves to be the descendants of the Chichimecs and the Otomi who fought against each other and whose peace is celebrated twice each year by the linking of the patron saint fiestas of Cruz del Palmar in January and San Luis de la Paz in August.

The presence of La Malinche in the song sung in this region might be interpreted as an actual historical event. Cortés gave his companion Malinche in marriage to a conquistador, Juan Jaramillo, with whom she had a child. Here is what a former fiesta leader from Cruz del Palmar, now deceased, explained to us: "Queen Malinche was Otomi, from here, she fell in love with Cortés, then came the family and she taught us to speak Spanish, thus our ancestry is Spanish. Cuauhtemoc was Otomi, he lived in the Montezuma mountain. This is what the old folks say" (*La reina Malinche era otomi, de aquí, se enamoró de Cortés, ya salió la familia y nos enseñó a hablar español. Así nuestra ascendencia es español. Cuauhtemoc era otomi, vivía en el cerro Montezuma. Así decían los viejillos*).[2]

"Lord of Villaseca" (*Señor de Villaseca*) is a favorite song performed during vigils. It is composed of twenty-two stanzas of four verses each, with a very regular rhythmic and rhyme scheme. Stanza one announces that the Lord of Villaseca saved a married woman; the song ends with the same text (stanza twenty-two).

> Year eighteen hundred
> ninety-one had been counted.
> The Lord of Villaseca
> saved a married woman.
>
> *Año de mil ochocientos*
> *noventa y uno contaba.*
> *El señor de Villaseca*
> *libró a una mujer casada.*

The following stanzas tell the story of this woman involved in an adulterous relationship. They describe how, after her husband left for work, she prepared a basket of food to bring to her lover. But unfortunately, says the song, she encountered her husband (*a su marido encontró*), who was upset and suspicious and called his wife an ungrateful woman (*a dónde vas mujer ingrata*) (stanza five). In answer to his query as to where she was going, she said, with her lips drying up (*que los labios se la secan*) (stanza six), that she was going to bring flowers to the Lord of Villaseca. When her husband raised the cloth of the basket with the tip of his dagger, miraculously the tortillas were flowers, the salt shaker was a resin burner (stanza eight), and the spoon had become a candle (stanza nine). The basket then contained exactly what people usually take as offerings to saints. As people told us and we observed, a saint needs his flowers, his resin, and his candles (*sus florecitas, su copal, y sus velas*).

In stanza ten the reassured husband tells his wife, as if he suspected the truth, that is, the adulterous behavior of his wife:

> Go take the flowers
> to that divine Lord
> and tell him to forgive
> the sins within our hearts.

> *Anda y llévale las flores*
> *a ese divino señor*
> *y dile que nos perdone*
> *las faltas del corazón.*

Then the woman went to a convent and knelt down in front of the door. The Lord crowned her with flowers. Inside the convent, she knelt down again and again received a crown of flowers (stanzas eleven and twelve).

Stanza thirteen states that a man also entered the convent and knelt down. Consequently the Lord of Villaseca decided not to kill the woman.

> Inside the gates
> the man knelt down
> ·the Lord of Villaseca
> removed his intent.

> *De las puertas para adentro*
> *el hombre se arrodilló*

49

*el Señor de Villaseca*
*el intento le quitó.*

Stanza fourteen ironically introduces the devil, who enjoys the foibles of a married woman:

And the devil who doesn't sleep
lives from his adventures
rejoices in the tricks
of a married woman.

*Y el diablo que no duerme*
*vive de sus aventuras*
*en una mujer casada*
*goza de sus travesuras.*

The final stanzas evoke the remembrances of the miracle of the Lord who saved the adulterous woman. This quaintly misogynist tale, which captures an authoritarian husband and a cunning wife, suggests that a married woman can be deceptive but good, that is, the Lord, triumphs over evil, that is, the devil. The Lord saved the woman from both her husband's wrath and sinning. The story told in the song took place in Cata in Guanajuato. Today this church in Cata has a crucifix called Señor de Villaseca, and the saint has the reputation of helping schoolchildren get good grades. They pray to him and, if successful, they bring him a copy of their grade report.

"The Musicians Go Two by Two" (*Van los concheros dos en dos*) is a short song made up of ten verses organized into two stanzas. The verses list the items that play an important part in this popular religion, the resin (copal), the resin burner (somador), the musicians (concheros) who play the armadillo shell, the flowers (florecitas), the altarpiece (ramillete), and the desert spoon (la cucharilla). The song is a verbal rendering in miniature of what is needed during the vigil.

The use of the diminutives copalito and florecitas expresses an intimate and simple endearment.

"The Year Nineteen Hundred" (*Año de mil nuevecientos*) refers to the period after the end of the Mexican Revolution when President Calles and the Catholic Church were in conflict (1926–1929). As is reported in history, the song says that the churches of the state of Guanajuato were torn down (stanza one). In stanza two the priest of Celaya announces that the church is going to be destroyed and proposes hiding its relics in another church. He says how much our hearts are hurting (stanza four):

> The priest of Celaya was saying
> how much our hearts hurt.
>
> *Decía el cura de Celaya*
> *como duele el corazón.*

Stanzas five and six state that the bishop of Morelia warned the city of Celaya that a church was going to be destroyed, and stanza seven says that the destruction took place with the help of the federal government. It is not surprising that, given the faith, religiosity, and respect for the Church of the people of this region, they sing a song on this topic. The song could be interpreted as an expression of the faith of the people called *Cristeros,* who defended the church during these events. Note that the singers do not use the standard Spanish word *novecientos* but instead *nuevecientos.*

"The Lord of Esquipula" (*Señor de Esquipula*) is a ballad (corrido)-like song composed of twelve stanzas. The song praises a black Christ. It says that a married man found this black Christ and brought it to his wife. The wife, referred to as "the ungrateful woman," burned the crucifix at ten o'clock in the morning, and at twelve noon she became a wolf forever. Her constant howling frightened the town. The song praises God and the crucifix, saying (stanza nine):

> You are like the moon
> you are like the sun
> you lighten us
> with your shining light.
>
> *Pareces la luna*
> *pareces el sol*
> *tú nos iluminas*
> *con tu resplandor.*

The song ends by saying that the Lord chose the city of Querétaro for his abode. Esquipulas is actually in Guatemala, but a replica of the black Christ of Esquipulas is kept in the sacristy of the church of Cruz de los Milagros in the town of Querétaro. For this reason the song says that the replica of the black Christ chose Querétaro city for its home.

"Star of the East" (*Estrella del Oriente*) has heterogeneous content, mingling religion and history in its sixteen stanzas. Stanza one says "it is time that we follow the path of the cross" (*ya es hora que sigamos el camino de la Cruz*). The holy cross is honored in this region like a saint, and it has its grandiose fiesta on May 22 in the Valle de Maiz neighborhood of San Miguel de Allende. In stanzas two through five, the four cardinal directions are associated with winds and saints, and they enjoin listeners to action by saying, in each stanza, "we must conquer" (*debemos conquistar*), possibly implying that in getting closer to the wind, believers would get closer to the saint. Stanza two links the east, the first wind, and the soul of Saint John. Stanza three links the west, the second wind, and the soul of Saint Luke. Stanza four links the south, the third wind, and the soul of Saint Matthew. Stanza five links the north, the fourth wind, and the soul of Saint Mark. Again, just as in the song "With Permission from God the Father" (*Con licencia de Dios Padre*), the prehispanic Four Winds and the Four Evangelists are associated as equal benefic entities. Again history is interpreted anachronistically and in very idiosyncratic and uncanny ways.

In stanza six Malinche flagellates herself, like a Christian martyr. In stanza seven Cuauhtemoc and even Charles V (1517–1556) and Queen Isabel of Spain, called here Malinche Isabel, appear. Stanza eight enjoins the listeners to perfume the Four Winds with the resin burner, to kiss one another's hands, and to say "He is God" (*El es Dios*), which perhaps signifies that everyone has been converted.

> Let us perfume the Four Winds
> with this copal burner
> let us kiss each other's hands
> and say "He is God."

> *Somemos los Cuatro Vientos*
> *con este somador*
> *y besémonos las manos*
> *y digamos "El es Dios."*

In stanza nine, the general, presumably Cortés, says, "Let us love one another." In stanzas eleven and twelve Cortés exhorts the Indians to fight the Turks, who are against Christianity. This scene is the epitome of anachronisms. The Spaniards had indeed fought the Turks, and no doubt the soldiers and friars had stories about battles in which they defended Christianity, and such tales captured the imagination of the recently converted Indians, who also pictured themselves as defenders of Christianity. Stanza thirteen describes the weapons of the people fighting for religion.

> Slingshots and arrows
> are all ready.
> Arrows fly through the wind
> fighting for religion.

> *Las hondas y las flechas*
> *ya todas en prevención.*
> *Al viento van las jaras*
> *peleando la religión.*

Stanza fifteen refers to the sad night (*Noche Triste*), the episode in the conquest of Mexico when Cortés was defeated and expelled from Tenochtitlán. He is supposed to have wept under a huge tree where he spent the night after his defeat. The last stanza refers to Tlaxcala, where Cortés found allies. Tlaxcala had been an enemy of the Aztecs. In Tlaxcala the defenders of the frontiers were Otomi warriors who also became allies of Cortés. Cruz del Palmar owns an ancient cross supposed to have come from Tlaxcala. "The general word" (*La palabra general*) refers to all the traditions preserved in the popular religion of the region.

These songs are examples of poetry transmitted from parents to children. They display the beliefs of the people and their own rendering of the history of the conquest, and especially their strong belief in Christianity and their religious fervor. They describe the conquest as a benefic event that introduced the Christian religion, and not as a humiliation and subjugation brought about by the military defeat. They praise the ancestors, the conqueror souls (*las ánimas conquistadoras*) who accepted the Christian faith and converted people around them so that Christianity has been transmitted through generations. The songs celebrate the conquest, conversion, and the Christian religion, and they honor the saints and the departed souls, and they often associate prehispanic and European Catholic beliefs and practices. No doubt people enjoy singing these ballads and hymns because of the type of characters who are the protagonists, everyday people, men and women, as well as saints, soldiers, and warriors. Elements of magical realism add suspense and excitement.

## VIGILS FOR THE FIESTA OF CRUZ DEL PALMAR

Several vigils are held from night into morning in honor of Holy Burial (Santo Entierro): On December 29–30 in San Luis de la Paz, on December 30–31 in Cruz del Palmar, when the vigil of the flower (velación de la flor) and the vigil of the desert spoon (velacion de la cucharilla) take place, and on January 5–6, when a vigil honors the fiesta officials (cargueros). While in Cruz del Palmar for the fiesta the visitors from San Luis de la Paz participate in several vigils as well.

Reaffirming every year the link between Cruz del Palmar and San Luis de la Paz, a vigil in honor of Holy Burial occurs during the night of December 28–29 in San Luis de la Paz. This vigil is held in the house of the fiesta leader (mayordomo) of the board of Holy Burial and is attended by neighbors and friends, as well as by people from la Misión, the Chichimec neighborhood of San Luis de la Paz. For the 1997 vigil we attended, the fiesta leaders and musicians came from Cruz del Palmar. People brought shrines of the two saints involved, Holy Burial and Saint Louis. This vigil was very similar in structure to the vigils of Cruz del Palmar and others we have participated in in the region, for example in San Miguel de Allende. People came to sing to and honor Holy Burial. They were ritually cleansed, and were offered food and drink. The Chichimecs from La Misión neighborhood spoke their language among themselves.

Two simultaneous vigils, the vigil of the flower (la velación de la flor) and the vigil of the desert spoon (la velación de la cucharilla), on the night of December 30–31, mark the beginning of the fiesta in Cruz del Palmar. At the vigil of the flower people bring flowers that will be taken to the procession the next day. People arrive at the vigil with fresh white flowers brought in large bunches. As the evening progresses, a profusion of flowers in large vats decorate the room, in front of and on the sides of the altar. The vigils of the flower in which we participated were held in a small room of a house compound. They began between 9 and 10 p.m. as people gradually arrived for the event. A group of individuals stood outside a small room of the house compound. Women served a hot drink made with cinnamon. The musicians entered the house and began tuning their instruments, talking and joking among themselves and with the slowly gathering group of visitors. In addition to the armadillo shell, their instruments included a guitar, a mandolin, and a banjo. Women sat against the walls of the small room. On the altar in the room the various offerings included flowers, resin (copal), Coca-Cola, a bottle of rubbing alcohol, and two large candles, as well as various saints and pictures, both on the altar and on the walls.

In the vigil of the flower in which we took part in 2000, the local priest opened the ceremony. He put on his cassock and stayed for a half-hour and prayed for the success of the event. After his departure the singing of ballads alternated with the cleansing of the participants. The leader of the musicians was the ritual leader of the vigil, the master of ceremonies. He led the participants in the ceremony of the Four Winds in which everyone turns in the four cardinal directions. Participants moved forward and were ritually cleansed by the master of ceremonies, who stood in front of the altar, while the musicians played. People who brought flowers were cleansed with them. During pauses women served tamales and bread, along with hot atole and Coca-Cola mixed with alcohol. There was much joking during these pauses. All the while a group of men outside the room, in the open of the quite cold night, were making the altarpiece. After they finished their work, they came into the room to be ritually cleansed with the altarpiece itself. Increasingly during this event, both inside and out, there was joking and drinking. As the evening proceeded, the joking became more and more intense and full of innuendos, metaphors, and allusions.

At the same time as the vigil of the flowers takes place in a private house, the vigil of the desert spoon takes place in a room on the side of the parish church. This vigil honors and blesses the desert spoon, the ritual plant that plays so important a role in the fiesta, being used to make the altarpieces and the adorned panels. It is fascinating that a room in the church, the central place of worship in the official Catholic religion, is also used for this popular religious ritual. The unfolding of events is essentially the same as in the vigil of the flowers, with an altar on one side of the room bearing images of saints, candles, and other objects. On another side of the room men construct the altarpiece. In the vigils in which we participated, the singing of hymns and ballads was accompanied by a guitar played by the master of ceremonies of this event, the fiesta leader; there was no group of musicians. The fiesta leader also cleansed the participants and made a speech at the end of the event, explaining its importance (for excerpts of this speech in Spanish and English, see appendix B2). He noted that the construction of the altarpiece was completed, and in the name of the fiesta officials he gave thanks to God, the Holy Virgin, and all the saints in the church of Cruz del Palmar for making this task possible:

> Well, dear ritual kin, now we have finished the work of making this altar-piece, as you see. For all of us, for all the fiesta officials, hoping God our Lord, the most holy Virgin, and all the other images that accompany [us] all around, we give thanks.

*Bueno, queridos compadritos, ya terminamos el trabajo de hacer ese ramillete, ustedes lo ven. Por todos nosotros, por todos los cargueros, esperando que Dios nuestro señor y la Santísima Virgen y demás imágenes que la acompañan alrededor, damos las gracias.*

He pointed out that every year people die and can no longer participate in the fiesta:

> Until next year when, God willing, we will be here, those of us who may be alive. For the sake of God, because life, from one moment to the next the end will come to each of us.

> *Hasta el venidero, si Dios nos da licencia, estaremos en este lugar, los que vivamos, sea por Dios, porque la vida, de un rato a otro nos llegará nuestro fin a cada quien.*

He honored by name the departed souls of previous fiesta officials and people in the community recently deceased, preposing José (for men) and María (for women) before each name.

Another vigil which takes place in Cruz del Palmar, during the night of January 5–6, is the vigil of the fiesta officials (cargueros), the culmination of the ceremony of selecting new officials for the following year. One of the years we saw it, it took place in a room on the side of the parish church. It was attended by three musicians, the ritual leader (mayordomo), the newly selected officials and their wives, and a female ritual leader (tenancha). Next to one wall was an altar. The event began with the singing of a hymn (*alabanza*) consisting of four stanzas. Stanza one addresses Holy Burial (called Santo Entierrito in the song). Stanza two addresses Jesus the Nazarene (Jesús Nazareno). Stanza three addresses the Holy Virgin (Santísima Virgen). Stanza four addresses the Holy Cross (Santísima Cruz). Each stanza speaks directly to the saint, using the familiar form *tu* and telling the saint that the believers are kneeling at his or her feet and begging the saint not to forget this sinner. Here is the first stanza (see appendix B3 for the full text in Spanish and English).

> Oh Holy Burial as you see it,
> here we have prostrated ourselves at your feet.
> Oh Holy Burial as you see it,
> here we have prostrated ourselves at your feet.
> For this reason I ask you, Father of my love,
> not to throw this sinner into oblivion.

*Ay Santo Entierrito como tú lo ves,*
*aquí nos ponemos postrados a tus pies.*
*Ay Santo Entierrito como tú lo ves,*
*aquí nos ponemos postrados a tus pies.*
*Por eso te pido, Padre de mi amor,*
*que no eches al olvido a este pecador.*

The hymn was followed by other songs. The musicians accompanied the singers on four instruments, a guitar, a mandolin, an armadillo shell, and a banjo. While the singing went on, two men redecorated altarpieces with fresh desert spoon. These altarpieces were the ones that had originally been made at the vigil of the desert spoon, the night of December 30–31.

At about three o'clock in the morning, the fiesta leader cleansed and purified the three musicians, the female ritual leader, and the ground with resin. Then he took one of the altarpieces and made the sign of the cross with it in front of the altar and blessed the two men who had redecorated the altarpieces. He then rested this altarpiece on the ground. He took the second altarpiece, made the sign of the cross with it in front of the altar and over the three selected officials, and presented it to each of them to kiss. Then he put this altarpiece on the ground where it had been and the officials returned to their places. While all this was going on the female ritual leader, holding her red flag (la pasión), had been ringing her little bell. At this point she hung her flag on the altar and stopped ringing the bell.

The vigil ended with speeches by the fiesta leader and one of the officials. In this concluding speech the fiesta leader stated that the duties pertaining to the worship of the saint were carried out according to tradition. He thanked the officials who helped pray for "Our Father, the Lord Holy Burial, Our Lord Father Jesus of Nazareth and Our Lady of Sorrows." He then expressed hope that during the night, God would ensure that people would decide to become officials for the following year. He reminded the gathering that life is borrowed and that death arrives for the old and the young. He ended his speech by thanking his ritual kin and the armadillo shell players:

For our part, thank you compadritos, players of the armadillo shell, who are here mainly to accompany the fiesta officials, and the fiesta official, who is both fiesta official and armadillo shell player.

*Por nuestra parte, muchísimas gracias compadritos, concheros, que acompañan*
*aquí a los cargueros principalmente, y el carguero quien es carguero y conchero*
*a la vez.*

Then the fiesta official ended the ceremony with an impressive list, including souls from purgatory, souls of ritual female specialists who bequeathed the traditions in honor of the saints, souls of officials, here called sargents, who founded the church Cruz del Palmar and lit the first resin burner and succeeded in erecting the church, which is today a parish. Here is this very poetic text (excerpts of this speech in Spanish and English are in appendix B4):

> In the name of the departed souls, those in purgatory mainly, all of those souls, the female ritual leaders, who with abundant tears left us these traditions, the sargents, who came to lay the first stone, where they kindled their fires to light their resin burner, where they then shed tears, such sargents who lay the holy stone where we stand now in this church, now a parish church.

> *A nombre de todas las ánimas, las del purgatorio principalmente, todas aquellas almas, aquellas tenanchas, que con tantas lágrimas nos dejaron estas santas tradiciones, aquellos sargentos, que vinieron a poner la primera piedra, en donde prendieron su lumbre para prender su somador, en donde aquellos entonces derramaron sus lágrimas, aquellos sargentos, por plantar esta santa piedra donde estamos hoy, en esta parroquia que hoy es parroquia.*

The vigil that occurs during the changing of duties represents the beginning of the closure to the fiesta, as it is the last vigil of the fiesta in Cruz del Palmar. It establishes continuity with past and future patron saint fiestas and with life in the community.

While in Cruz del Palmar, the visitors from San Luis de la Paz participate in vigils with the people who host them, and thus the links between the two places are reaffirmed. People in Cruz del Palmar remember that in previous times there were more vigils, for example for the stick rockets (*cohetes*), which are important elements in the fiesta during the many processions. Formerly there were also a board (*mesa*) and slaves (*esclavos*) who were initiated, but this practice was discontinued because the priests objected to it.

### VIGILS FOR THE FIESTA OF SAN LUIS DE LA PAZ

The official day of the fiesta of Saint Louis (San Luis Rey) in San Luis de la Paz is August 25. Before and after August 25 a series of interspersed vigils take place in San Luis de la Paz and La Misión, the Chichimec neighborhood.

On August 22, in the morning, people from La Misión gather the desert spoon (cucharilla) that will be used to embellish the adorned panel (here called a chimal). That night a vigil is held in a house in La Misión that has been used for generations for vigils and where there is a small chapel. During the vigil men prepare the desert spoon.

What follows is a description of a series of events Yolanda Lastra observed in 1999, representative of the general sequence of events that take place in and around San Luis de la Paz. On August 23, the fiesta leaders (mayordomos), the female ritual leader (tenancha), and some members of the community of Cruz del Palmar arrived in San Luis de la Paz and went to the chapel of San Ignacio, a neighborhood of San Luis. The visitors from Cruz del Palmar were greeted by the people of San Ignacio, and that evening they participated in a vigil. The fiesta leaders of Cruz del Palmar played music and sang. The guests were offered hot drinks and tamales by the hosts of San Ignacio. This vigil, bringing together the visitors from Cruz del Palmar and the people from San Luis and La Misión, was similar in structure to those vigils we have already described.

On the morning of August 26, the day after the celebrations for Saint Louis of August 25, the slaves (esclavos) devoted to Santo Entierro and San Luisito went to get the saints (demanditas, santitos) in the church of San Luisito and carried them to the house of the first leader of the board of Holy Burial (mayordomo de la mesa de Santo Entierro). They put them on an altar adorned with flowers and candles in the following order, from left to right: San Luisito from La Misión, the santos médicos from Cruz del Palmar, Holy Burial from San Luis de La Paz, Holy Burial from Cruz del Palmar, Holy Burial from La Misión, and San Luisito from Cruz del Palmar. These saints, thus grouped, are an expression of the intimate ritual relationship that exists among these places, Cruz del Palmar, San Luis de la Paz, and La Misión. All day the slaves of Holy Burial remained with the saints. It is said that they accompany (acompañan) the saints. At night a vigil took place. We describe this vigil in detail below.

The next day, August 27, the saints were transported in procession to another house for a visit (posada) where they would be cared for and where there would be a vigil as well. That year, 1999, on August 27, 28, 29, and 30 and on September 2 and 12, vigils took place in different houses to which the saints had been moved for visits. This series of vigils takes place every year.

Here is a detailed description of the August 26 vigil, which shows the complex structure of vigils and their potential political significance. The room was decorated with hanging crêpe paper and balloons. Some of the balloons had confetti inside. The altar took up almost the entire wall at the back of the room, except for a little place on each side that was used for children to sleep. Mats were spread on the ground. The altar was covered with a plastic tablecloth and it was obvious that that this was a permanent altar, because of the quantity of small paintings, photographs, and reproductions (*cuadritos* and *estampitas*) of saints. Some decorations of colored tissue paper covered part of the wall. The saints appeared in the usual order and included an extra Holy Burial on the extreme right. The people attending the vigil entered and crossed themselves in front of the altar. Some stayed in the room where the altar was located, but the majority remained in the patio, seated on benches. Later the second fiesta leader from la Misión arrived with his older son. The fiesta leader of Cruz del Palmar threw resin in one of the burners and performed the Four Winds ceremony.

After a while music began. This time it included two guitars and an armadillo shell. In addition, various women from Cruz del Palmar and San Luis de la Paz sang, as did some younger people. The majority of the children went out to play in the street. The musicians began to play, and the fiesta leader perfumed the saints and the Earth many times with resin smoke, performing the ceremony of the Four Winds with all the participants. The female ritual leader rang her bell. They sang to Santiago, the messenger of the Four Winds (correo de los Cuatro Vientos), and invoked the souls of the deceased slaves or fiesta leaders of the house. Singing went on during the entire night, with interruptions to drink beverages and smoke. The owner of the house constantly put cigarettes on a small plate in front of the altar for people. Everyone seemed happy. Greetings and news were exchanged, and there was much joking. As usual in these vigils, children and old people sat or fell asleep, wrapped up in blankets.

That particular evening the vigil took on a special character. Three clay plates, one with salt, another with earth, and a third one with ashes, and two resin burners (somadores) with embers rested on the altar. Before the altar a tray bearing a fruit bowl—mainly bananas and apples, with some pomegranates—rested on the ground. It became evident that this display had been planned in relation to the content of the speech that was to be given during the evening.

The ritual specialist from Cruz del Palmar stood up, then read and commented on an anonymous text he had acquired in Xichu in the Sierra Gorda mountains. Xichu has the reputation of being an important center of the popular traditions associated with honoring the saints. To have been to Xichu and to refer to it is a significant rhetorical move on the part of the ritual leader. In so doing he confers legitimacy and authenticity on his own words. The cosmology and the symbolism of his speech are a mixture of Catholic and indigenous elements and are punctuated by pauses during which he said, "He is God" (*El es Dios*), to which the audience responded, "He is God," thus forming a tight community of participants jointly expressing their devotion.

The ritual leader began by informing the audience of the existence of a group of faithful from Xichu that decided to participate in the festivities in honor of Friar San Miguel, the founder of San Miguel de Allende, whose spirit is still with the people of the region. Referring to the tradition of the Sierra Gorda, he then talked about the altar erected during vigils and about the cross. Using a poetic metaphor, he said that the altar contained offerings "to our loved ones, who preceded us on the trip which has no return" (*a nuestros seres queridos, que se nos adelantaron en el viaje que no tiene retorno*). Without elaborating, he said that the altar is composed of three planes that represent the three dimensions of the earth, and he noted that the cross with its two intersecting parts is a symbol of cosmic forces.

Then the ritual leader proceeded to talk about five crosses that "indicate our steps in the world" (*indican nuestros pasos por este mundo*). He said that the cross of salt (*la cruz de sal*) is what preserves individuals in this world and enables them to accomplish their mission on Earth. He explained that salt preserves bodies and prevents rot. At this point he informed the audience that girls would walk around offering salt, which tells God that the ceremony under way is sacred. Then he explained that the cross of earth (*la cruz de tierra*) symbolizes the bosom of our mother, who gives us food and sustains our thought. According to the ritual leader, the cross of ashes (*la cruz de ceniza*) is a symbol of our matter, which must go back to Earth. The ritual leader said that the priests also tell us that we are of ashes and to ashes we must return (*"ceniza somos y a ceniza tenemos que llegar"*).

After discussing the three crosses — salt, earth, and ashes — the ritual leader got to the fourth, the cross of flowers (*la cruz de las flores*), which is the one that people deserve for their good work and which leads to the fifth cross, the cross of light (*la cruz de la luz*). He elaborated that this cross is the symbol of divinity, of the center, of the internal fire that makes us human. This notion of fire led him to refer to the burning of resin (copal), which, he said, allows the faithful who use it to consume their tears and to offer pleasant perfumes to the giver of life (*"que nos permite por medio de copal consumir nuestras lágrimas y ofrecerlas en aromas agradables al dador de la vida"*). The ritual leader emphasized that all the traditions he had been talking about are sacred (*"Todo esto es una cosa sagrada en nuestras tradiciones"*).

At this point, the ritual leader referred to the plates with food and fruit in front of the altar and said they were for the body and for humanity. Changing the topic abruptly, he added that vigils are always accompanied by a choral group whose music is used to request benevolence from the spirit. The specialist then commented that right then, the musicians were participating in the ceremony, singing hymns to the Lord, adoring him according to his traditions. He ended his speech by saying, "That is what these things mean" (*Eso es lo que significan estas cosas*) and cautioning that no one should "misinterpret and (accuse us) of doing other things" (*para que no vayan a interpretar mal, que vamos a hacer otras cosas*). This was a plea (indirectly addressed to priests, who tend to dismiss these practices as idolatry) not to misinterpret the behavior of the believers in this honoring of the saints.

The plates with earth, salt, and ashes on the altar, the fruit tray on the ground, and the resin burners were displayed there as concrete manifestations of what the speech expressed. When the ritual leader finished speaking, a young girl picked up the small plate containing salt from the altar and took it around in the room. Everyone took a pinch of salt and made the sign of the cross. The ritual leader then perfumed the fruit in the bowl in front of the altar with the resin burner, and distributed it. Afterward the hosts served bread and coffee. Then the people continued singing ballads until dawn. The event concluded with the singing of Catholic prayers. Finally, people took leave of one another.

This moving speech enabled the ritual leader to reiterate and emphasize the significance of the practices and beliefs manifested in vigils and in patron saint fiestas more generally (excerpts of this speech in Spanish and English are in appendix B). While the speech might seem a bit esoteric and obscure to readers, it reflects and expresses the deep religiosity and the sincere conviction of these people. Remarks about the significance and importance of these celebrations are often expressed during or at the end of vigils, in much simpler and less obtuse terms than in the speech we have discussed in detail here.

Vigils are expressions of religious devotion and fervor, combined with a sense of intimacy, among family, neighbors, friends, visitors, and especially saints. The beauty created by the flowers, musical performances and singing, offerings, and gradual construction of the altarpiece (ramillete) or the adorned panel (crucero) makes these events magnificent examples of communitas.[3] The collective performance of hymns and ballads, with their phonic and semantic repetitions and parallelisms, rhythms, assonances and consonances, and distinctive voice qualities relating the past to the present give power to the voices that performers and listeners share. The spaces in which events take place—the courtyard, the bedroom, the kitchen—are transformed from domestic spaces into sites of sacred and ritual celebration. The scents, the exuberant visual displays, the rhythms of the music, the poetry of the singing, and the intimacy of the people crowded together create a mystical sociability. Participants are engaged in a sensory and sensual atmosphere of sounds, sights, smells, tastes, and movements, a constellation that takes one outside the realm of the ordinary.

The speeches in particular play an important role. Again and again, fiesta leaders, specialists, and officials point out that the vigil, with its altar and offerings, singing, Four Wind ceremonies, resin to perfume the saints, sacred objects, and cleansing and purification of participants, is "our" tradition, transmitted by the ancestors to the present day, and needs to be preserved and continued. Similar references to mortality and to the ancestors are frequently made in speeches, songs, and actions. During patron saint fiestas processions always make a point of visiting the cemetery of the community. Again and again, speakers defend these customs as genuine forms of worship. They display a strong sense of religiosity and respect for the saints. Along with the religious message there is a performative enactment and indeed action, a collective political affirmation that "our" traditions must be continued and must be respected.

FIGURE 3.1
*Musicians playing an armadillo shell (concha) and mandolin during a vigil.*
*Photograph by Joel Sherzer.*

FIGURE 3.2
*Musicians and singers performing during a vigil. Photograph by Yolanda Lastra.*

FIGURE 3.3
*Ritual meal (*reliquia*) in San Luis de la Paz. Photograph by Yolanda Lastra.*

FIGURE 3.4
*Ritual meal dishes prepared for newly selected fiesta officials in Cruz del Palmar.
Photograph by Yolanda Lastra.*

# FOUR

# PROCESSIONS, ENCOUNTERS, CEREMONIES, AND MASSES

## (*Procesiones, encuentros, ceremonias, y misas*)

Religious celebrations in Mexico are famous for their spectacular processions, involving a profusion of flowers, pageantry, music, and costumes, with huge crowds moving along and many spectators watching. Patron saint fiestas are one of the occasions for such elaborate processions. Large processions carry, indeed display and honor, the saints with elaborate pageantry. It is believed that by their presence, the saints will bring protection and good fortune to the places and spaces visited. In the region we study here, around San Miguel de Allende, Cruz del Palmar, and San Luis de la Paz, other processions, smaller and more intimate, accompany officials going to a calvary or a church to request permission to hold the fiesta. Small processions are also central to the conduct of other fiesta ritual activities. In this case the processions provide the appropriate decorum and respect.

Patron saint processions have their own set of protocols and practices. At the head of a procession in this region, whether big or small, the same set of elements must be present. Typically an official carries a banner with the name of the community and a representation of its saint. A ritual leader carries the resin burner (somador). He is accompanied by the female ritual leader (tenancha), who has in her hands sacred paraphernalia consisting of a red flag (la pasión) and a small bell (campanita) that she constantly rings. Others carry saints or sacred objects, such as crosses and altarpieces (ramilletes), or flowers and candles. Replicas of the saints in small shrines or pictures of the saints are in a place of prominence at the head of the procession. Followers of their cult transport them through streets and up and down hills, from one house to another, from one church to another, and from one ritual space to another, stopping at important sacred locations such as churches, cemeteries, calvaries, and the homes of ritual leaders and others who want to honor the saint. Such individuals have their houses decorated and may have made a promise (manda) to honor the saint.

In all patron saint processions, big or small, a medley of sounds and noises fills the air, adding to the excitement of the occasion. Musicians are an integral component. In larger processions many musicians in brass bands (bandas) play brass and percussion instruments, which provide the basic tempo, and reed instruments, which alternate in the lead. They perform nineteenth-century military music, including marches, waltzes, and polkas, always in a major key. Mariachis may also be part of a procession, playing well-known traditional Mexican songs. Sometimes two musicians, called *tunditos,* come from the Sierra Gorda, a nearby mountain range. Dressed in white and wearing sandals, they play flutes (*chirimias*) and drums. They belong to an ancient tradition and play strident indigenous music. In small processions there are two or three musicians playing the violin, trumpet, and drum.

Men walking along with the processions detonate stick rockets (cohetes). Their duty is to explode the rockets as long as the procession lasts. When the procession arrives at the community church, church bells ring loudly. The low bells are steady, the higher bells provide a counterrhythm.

The visual and aural experience of a procession, already quite extraordinary, is enhanced by the many groups of dancers, accompanied by musicians, participating to honor the saints. Typically, groups of rattle dancers (*danzantes de sonajas*) are a feature of the patron saint procession in the immediate region around San Miguel de Allende. Children ages five to twelve or older wear straw hats decorated by their mothers with paper flowers and ribbons. They are well-dressed, in their best attire. They have an air of propriety and innocence about them.

In this region, French and Apache (Franceses y Apaches) or French and Chichimec (Franceses y Chichimecas) dance groups, as well as plumed dancers (*danzantes de pluma* or *concheros*), also participate in processions. Designers and choreographers who work with these groups create costumes on the basis of images they have seen in books and other performances. French soldiers sometimes wear blue uniforms and a kepi. Apaches and Chichimecs have painted faces and might wear animal skins and various body adornments. Plumed dancers wear elaborate and lavish headdresses. The dancers—men, women, and children—represent imagined Indians, thus bringing an indigenous component to fiestas.

Crazies (locos) are increasingly present in processions in the region around San Miguel de Allende. They are cross-dressed individuals who wear Halloween and carnival-type masks and costumes. Masks can be bought in local markets. In addition, we were told in Cruz del Palmar that "the kids went to the United States to buy the clothes" (*los chamacos fueron al norte a comprar la ropa*). Their masks are sometimes of easily identifiable figures, such as Raúl

Salinas, past and disgraced president of Mexico, Vicente Fox, George Bush, and other political figures; famous historical individuals, such as Emiliano Zapata; and cartoon and film characters, such as Bugs Bunny and the Pink Panther. They appear here and there during fiestas, wildly erotic and exotic, creative and innovative, hilariously funny, sarcastically and sardonically subversive. Yet at the same time they are not marginal to fiestas but very much a part of them. There seem to be more and more crazies at every fiesta we participate in. An enormous fiesta of crazies in San Miguel de Allende, in honor of Saint Anthony of Padua, centered in the neighborhood of his church, involves all of San Miguel. It is said that during this patron saint fiesta, "everybody in San Miguel becomes crazy" (*todo San Miguel es loco*).

Along with the crazies, men dressed as women and others parading as little bulls (toritos) prance around. The bulls are made of a semicylindrical wooden or cardboard structure covered with a cloth. The main axis of the structure protrudes forward and holds a mask of a bull. One such group, quite famous, comes from the town of Silao next to Leon.

Enormous puppets (mojigangas) often suddenly emerge during patron saint fiesta processions. Towering above other participants and bystanders, with their exaggerated breasts and behinds, deformed faces, and gaudy, colorful clothes, they are the epitome of bad taste. Given their enormous size, grotesque appearance, and attire, they are uncannily funny. The enormous puppets, like the crazies, are often itinerant groups contracted for the fiesta. Like the crazies, the puppets often include recognizable individuals. In May 2006, an enormous puppet of presidential candidate Andrés Manuel López Obrador appeared at a political rally in San Miguel de Allende. He stood next to the stage where the real candidate made his political speech at noon. In the evening the puppet (but not the real candidate) showed up at the patron saint fiesta in the neighborhood of the Valle de Maiz.

Strange costumed creatures, animals and others, can appear as well. Individuals on stilts (*zanco*), gorillas, devils, and parodies of political figures frequently join in and appear to have great fun, to the delight of bystanders.

Visitors and people from the community, including men, women, and children, in their best clothes, also walk in processions, carrying flowers, candles, and images of saints. These huge processions bring together large crowds of people, which are monitored very carefully by fiesta officials. These officials make sure that groups and people move along in an orderly fashion and that cars and buses can pass so that the traffic is not completely stopped. They also take care of the dancers, fixing a costume or bringing water and juice to people who march for hours under a hot sun.

During patron saint fiestas, it is common for encounters to take place between processions coming from another town or other neighborhood. Encounters in fiestas, in addition to their possible indigenous roots, may be related to the encounter of Christ on the way to Calvary with his mother. During these encounters people participate in long and elaborate ritual greetings in which they are perfumed with resin (copal) to purify them. For instance, people who have moved from the small village of La Cieneguita to San Miguel de Allende process back to their home village on their patron saint's day. Small processions from homes in which vigils have been held meet up with the main procession in Cruz del Palmar and again exchange ritual greetings and blessings. A procession from San Luis de la Paz comes to Cruz del Palmar during the Cruz del Palmar fiesta and joins the Cruz del Palmar procession outside the village in a ceremony that includes ritual greetings and blessings. A parallel encounter between the two communities occurs during the fiesta in San Luis de la Paz. These particular encounters between Cruz del Palmar and San Luis de la Paz are not mere happenstance; they are of great significance historically, politically, and religiously, and are a prominent moment in these fiestas.

Processions usually end at the church of the village or the town, where the priest welcomes the saint and the worshipers. Catholic priests participate only marginally and perfunctorily in patron saint fiestas, unlike the fiesta leaders and officials. However, priests do greet the parishioners when they come to church on the saint's day, and they preside over several masses during the fiesta. On the day of the saint, as well as at other times in the fiesta, they preside over high masses in honor of the saint. These masses may be more or less elaborate, depending on the place and the year, and may feature the local bishop or other church officials, in addition to the priest of the local church. Priests may also conduct masses to mark the beginning or end of the fiesta. They are generally active in a religious capacity during other moments of the fiesta, for example, granting permission to remove the saint from the church or presiding over the start of an all-night vigil.

In processions, ceremonies, encounters, and masses, entire communities are on display. People commune with one another as they honor their saints. Processions are noisy, bustling, and festive. They involve an extraordinary mingling of sounds, noises, and smells, as well as bright colors and movements. Dancers take pride in their costumes and body painting. Streets and highways are transformed into special spaces, and all usual activities are stopped. There is literally a taking over of the topography, hills, squares, paths, and streets, which become religious, symbolic places imbued with the presence of the saint and the participants. The procession route is marked by colorful strings of cutouts (papel picado) that are hung across the streets and in front of houses and stores. The leaders of the fiesta head up the processions. More generally, though, processions are not hierarchical and are not dominated by men. Men, women, old people, and children take part in the rites and gatherings, all expressing the religiosity and communion among people adoring their saints. Processions, encounters, ceremonies, and masses are festive and religious, and bring together the whole community in a common purpose.

## CRUZ DEL PALMAR

A succession of processions, encounters, ceremonies, and masses punctuates the patron saint fiesta of Cruz del Palmar. These events include, a month before the fiesta, the fiesta leader (mayordomo) and officials (cargueros) going in a small procession to request permission to hold the fiesta; a large procession within Cruz del Palmar meeting a procession from San Luis de la Paz in a ritual encounter on December 31; a high mass attended by many people on January 1, often in the courtyard of the parish church; a small procession for the promenade of the cow (paseo de la vaca) on January 5 in the morning; and a procession for the gathering of the breads (*recogida de panes*) the same evening. The changing of duties (cambio de cargos), celebrated on January 6, involves a procession, and on the final day, January 7, a huge procession marks the end of the fiesta. It takes six processions, several encounters, multiple ceremonies, and masses to honor Holy Burial.

### *The Permission Procession: November 27*

Whereas preparations for the fiesta of Cruz del Palmar begin when the officials for the following year are selected, on January 6, they commence on November 27, when the fiesta officials go in a procession to request permission to begin rehearsals to have the rattle (sonaja) dances in front of the church. The official in charge of these dances is at the head of the procession. He carries a reproduction of the patron saint of Cruz del Palmar, Holy Burial (Santo Entierro), in a shrine (demandita). To his right the female ritual leader carries her red banner and rings a tiny bell. To his left the fiesta leader (mayordomo) carries the resin burner (somador). Behind them follow four musicians. Two play drums and two play violins. A stick rocket man (cohetero) and a woman with a basket of flowers, candlesticks, and fennel accompany them. Behind them come the children who will be the dancers. The procession goes to the parish church, entering through the door on one side. They go to the little calvary (calvarito) in the atrium and then inside the church to the main altar and then to Justo Juez, a small image of Christ with a crown of thorns and clad in a purple robe on one of the walls of the church. Afterward they go out of the church and walk to the cemetery and pray for the ancestors. Then they stop again to pray for the ancestors at another little calvary situated on the way to the calvary on the hill. At this point the children receive flowers. After this pause, everyone goes up to the calvary on the hill, where the ritual leader directs the ceremony of the Four Winds with the resin burner, first standing up, then kneeling and perfuming the earth. After that the official formally asks permission to hold the dances. In a permission ceremony we observed, a ritual leader first announced he would ask permission from the Lord in Heaven to hold the dance, then he actually did so. He also referred to the conquering souls who adopted these traditions and who also asked permission to hold a fiesta:

> I am going to ask permission of the Lord in Heaven for the dance. Permission, Lord, I am about to assemble the ritual paraphernalia associated with the Lord Holy Burial of the calvary. I come back to ask for permission from the Holy Cross of the cemetery where the first fiesta official cried. He who left us this path. Here we are measuring the path, asking permission. Holy Cross of the Port of Calderón. Where the blessed souls sat to ask for permission, souls of the Four Winds, conquering souls who left the path, the gates of the Lord Holy Burial, Our Lady of Sorrows, the Lord of Humility.

> *Voy a pedir permiso por el señor de los Cielos para parar la danza. Permiso, señor, voy a dar la rosa que es la mesa del señor Santo Entierro del Calvario. Regreso para pedir permiso a la Santa Cruz del Camposanto donde lloró el primer carguero. Quien nos dejó este camino. Estamos aquí midiendo el camino, pidiendo permiso. Santa Cruz del Puerto de Calderón. Donde se sentaron las benditas ánimas para pedir el permiso, ánimas de los cuatro vientos, ánimas conquistadoras quienes dejaron el camino, las puertas del señor Santo Entierro, la Virgen de los Dolores, el señor de la Humildad.*

This short address, imbued with respect and fervor, invokes the ancestors and the saints, including the Holy Cross, adored as a saint in this region. After the request for permission to hold the fiesta is completed, the procession walks back to the parish church to return the saint. Now the rehearsals for the dances and other arrangements for the fiesta can take place (for the text of another permission request, see appendix C1).

## Procession to the Calvary, Parish Church, and Encounter: December 31

During the morning and early afternoon of December 31 a festive atmosphere permeates Cruz del Palmar. There is a dense overlapping of forms and modes of expression, costumes, music, dances, flowers, sounds, sights, and colors. Many people, well dressed, walk in the streets. Men work outside the house of the fiesta leader, putting the final touches on the adorned panel that will be carried in the procession. Costumed adolescents and children who are part of the French and Apache dance groups and the rattle dance groups jump, prance, move about, practice, and play around, as music is played. There is much talking, joking, and laughing. The event builds up to a crescendo. After a while the people working on the adorned panel, the dancers, and the musicians eat a meal together in the house of the fiesta leader. This is one of many ceremonial meals that occur during the fiesta.

At about three in the afternoon the adorned panel decorated with desert spoon (cucharilla) destined for the calvary on the hill is ready. The men pick it up and begin walking swiftly, almost running (because of the weight of the panel) up the hill toward the calvary. Behind them a procession forms. The French and Apache dancers and their musicians playing instruments make their way up the hill to the calvary. Young men take out a wooden crucifix from the calvary, and the door of the calvary is once again closed. The original crucifix in this calvary, a beautiful, ancient object of considerable value, was unfortunately stolen and has been replaced by a tapestry representing the crucifixion, thus adapting to the real world of the possibility of theft and maintaining the procession tradition with the use of a different object. After the crucifix or other representation of Christ on the cross has been taken out of the calvary, the adorned panel is erected in front of the calvary. This is no easy task, as the adorned panel is extremely heavy.

The crucifix is carried by several men at the head of the procession, which proceeds down the hill in the direction of the center of town. Now the procession grows and expands, as people come from all directions to join it. A group coming from the house where the vigil of the flowers was held the night before meets the procession coming from the calvary, which comes to a halt. This group is composed of a children's rattle dance group, shaking rattles, and their musical band, and some men carrying the altarpiece they made the night before and many white flowers, as well as a shrine containing Holy Burial. The two processions face each other and exchange ritual greetings and blessings, a precursor in form of the larger, more elaborate encounter to come. Other small processions come down to the main road and join the main procession, which becomes continually bigger and bigger and more and more boisterous. As each new procession joins the larger one, ritual greetings are exchanged. More and more dance and music groups enter in. The fiesta leader heads the procession, carrying his resin burner, along with his young son and the female ritual leader, who carries her red flag and rings her small bell. As the procession proceeds, stick rockets explode in the air. The French and Apache dancers create figures as they move along, inside and outside the procession, accompanied by Death (Muerte), the Devil (Diablo), and two Monkeys (Changos), who get involved in spectacular chasing and forays with French and Apaches (the costumes of this group are described in chapter five).

When the procession arrives in the center of town, it stops at the atrium of the parish church, where, in front of the church's closed doors, the various musical bands often play "Las Mañanitas," a popular Mexican song played on birthdays and other celebrations. At this point men lift up and carry the three large adorned panels that had been placed leaning against the church and join the procession. It takes at least ten men to carry the largest of these. Other people leave the church with small shrines of the saints and the *parande,* a wooden board, covered with a cloth and crêpe paper decorations. Loaves of bread wrapped in plastic are attached to the parande and will later be sold to raise money. At the end of the procession a brass band plays wind instruments.

Each year this procession descends through the street to the other side of town and across a large field, where it meets the procession coming from San Luis de la Paz. It is here that the encounter between these two groups, one from Cruz del Palmar of Otomi origin and one from San Luis de la Paz of Chichimec origin, takes place. When the two processions meet, they stop facing each another and about fifteen feet apart. The large adorned panels are set down on the ground under trees near the meeting place of the two processions, musicians stand on a nearby hill, and the encounter begins in a respectful silence. A solemn event is about to begin.

The two groups face one another. The leaders of the two communities stand in front of their respective processions facing one another and carry their saints, Holy Burial and Saint Louis. Other officials carry the banner representing their saints. The fiesta leader of Cruz del Palmar, on his knees, greets the visitors from San Luis. Then the leaders bless one another alternately with their resin burners and make the sign of the cross in front of the saints. The people from San Luis, behind their fiesta leader, carry red and white flowers, those from Cruz del Palmar, behind their fiesta leader, carry all white flowers. Then, over a period of several hours, the people from the two communities cross themselves and kiss both of the saints in shrines, Holy Burial and Saint

Louis. Women throw confetti. People from the village, visitors, the rattle dancers, and the French and Apache dancers participate in this enactment and demonstration of affection and fervor for the two saints, Holy Burial and Saint Louis.

This encounter is an extremely moving moment, reflecting the depth of the tradition involved. It is a manifestation as well as an enactment of respect for the saints and the human participants. It is spiritual and emotional, a re-affirmation of the link of peace between the two groups, Cruz del Palmar and San Luis de la Paz, and their respect for and honoring of each other's saint.

When the encounter is over, the two processions merge into a single huge procession and proceed back to town to the parish church. The procession gets larger and larger as many people join it to enter the church. People are patient, disciplined, and orderly. When the procession arrives at the church, it is headed by many people on their knees, who had made mandas, promises to Holy Burial, to ask for some favor or in penance. They lead the procession into the atrium toward the church, where they are greeted by the priest. Church bells ring slowly and loudly. All individuals in the procession enter the church, where the leaders place flowers, the small saints, and the altar-pieces on the floor in front of the altar. On each side of the entrance to the parish church men erect two large adorned panels; a third one is erected in front of the small calvary in the atrium. These panels had been transported to the encounter and were lying on the ground during the ceremony. The children's dance groups begin dancing, each group in front of their respective adorned panel, and families and friends sit and watch and talk. This procession, which began early in the afternoon ends, as the sun sets.

### The Promenade of the Cow (Paseo de la vaca): January 5 (morning)

The Spaniards introduced cattle and cattle culture into this region, and during fiestas in general and patron saint fiestas in particular, bullfights and rodeos take place in many communities. In Cruz del Palmar a striking procession takes place on January 5. This is the promenade of the cow. From December 31 to January 5, music, children's rattle dances in the parish church, and all-night vigils have gone on nonstop. The preparations for the procession begin about 8:30 a.m. A cow is placed in a pen outside the house of the official in charge of the event. He and his assistants put a wreath of vegetables, onion, carrots, garlic, and various greens around the neck of the cow, then walk with the cow in a procession through town, up to the calvary on the hill, to the cemetery, and to the parish church, where the cow is taken into the atrium. The Four Winds ceremony takes place at each of these stops. The Cruz del Palmar banner is part of the procession. A musical ensemble composed of two violinists and two drummers goes along with the cow, and the musicians play in a lively tempo in a major key. Some of the Indians from the Apache and French dance group also walk with their musicians. After the procession has walked through several streets, it returns to the courtyard of the house of the official in charge. All the participants drink rum and eat a meal of tortillas and beans served by the official in charge of this event and his family. Finally, after most people have left, the cow is slaughtered. Later it is cooked in a broth (*caldo*) to be served to the entire town, and to any visitors. While this event is part of the fiesta in Cruz del Palmar, the members of the community do not describe it as a sacrifice in honor of the saint (the origins of this practice are discussed in chapter six).

## Gathering of Breads (Recogida de panes): January 5

The upcoming Feast of the Epiphany in the Catholic Church calendar on January 6, involving consuming the bread of kings (*roscas de los reyes*), might explain the ritual gathering of breads that takes place on January 5 as part of the patron saint fiesta of Cruz del Palmar. This event entails a procession through the village during which the ritual offering and receiving of bread are a symbolic expression of the changing of fiesta officials.

On the evening of January 5, after a mass at about 6 p.m., a procession takes place. It begins with the fiesta leader and the female ritual leader entering the home where the visitors from San Luis de la Paz are staying. There they take the small saints belonging to Cruz del Palmar from the altar. The saints had been honored during the vigil held the previous night. The fiesta leader and the female ritual leader form a procession that goes to the homes of all the current officials of the fiesta. The purpose of this procession is the gathering of breads (recogida de los panes), and it is a preparation for the changing of duties (cambio de cargos). The breads are called breads of the kings (roscas de reyes), which, as in the European Catholic tradition, are in the shape of a circular crown and contain pieces of fruit or little statues representing the infant Jesus and are consumed at this time of year. The breads are purchased in San Miguel de Allende. They are made especially for the fiesta and are larger than the ones sold commercially.

The outgoing officials are required to offer bread to the incoming officials for the following year. In their house they have displayed the breads on boards covered with embroidered tablecloths. Sometimes people cover the breads with plastic bags. The result is a carefully prepared artistic presentation. In addition, the outgoing official must offer nine sticks of brown sugar (*nueve pilones de piloncillo*) to the new official.

When the procession, led by the fiesta leader, arrives at the house of each official, the owners of the house are waiting with their breads and sugar. The fiesta leader enters the house and perfumes the bread with resin; he is met by the outgoing official, who is standing with the breads and sugar. His wife stands with flowers and candles. In addition to the husband and wife, other members of the family come out of the house, along with ritual kin (compadres) and friends who helped the official fulfill his commitment. Each time the outgoing official and his party join the procession carrying the bread to the atrium of the parish church.

The procession is accompanied by a large and noisy brass band (banda). The French and Apache dancers follow the procession with their drumming band. They dance in front of each of the houses of the fiesta officials. As the procession nears each house, the stick-rocket men explode their stick rockets.

After visiting all of the houses of the officials, the procession finally reaches the square in the center of town, walks around it, then enters the atrium of the parish church. The breads are placed on tables and arranged in a parallel formation. The outgoing officials stand in line in front of the small calvary. Then these men and the French and Apache dancers enter the church and make the sign of the cross. They leave walking backward, and the dancers begin dancing as they walk out of the atrium. This is a beautiful ceremony, carefully choreographed, with every detail—the presentation and the display of the breads, the position of the dancers, and the grouping of the officials— helping to create an elegant, harmonious event in the night.

## Changing of Duties (Cambio de cargos): January 6

To ensure the continuity of traditions and the commitment of fiesta leaders and officials, a procession accompanied by various ceremonies takes place on January 6. It is called the changing of duties. The gathering of the breads leads to the changing of duties, which takes place the following evening, January 6. The broth made from the slaughtered cow that had been paraded through the town during the promenade of the cow and the breads that were collected during the gathering of bread procession become part of the ceremony of the changing of duties, a complex event that includes a ritual meal, procession, music, speeches, blessings, cleansings, and a vigil.

The evening begins festively, with a large band playing in the street in front of the atrium of the parish church. Sometimes enormous puppets dance in front of the band. The official and ritual part of the evening begins with a procession. The fiesta leader and his son leave their house and walk up the street to the parish church, carrying the broth made from the slaughtered cow. They meet others, carrying tortillas, and the procession enters the atrium and lines up in front of the altar across from the church, where the bread had been placed on tables the night before. Some of the broth is poured into twelve jars, which are lined up on the ground and covered with colored tortillas. The number twelve may refer to the twelve apostles. Next to the jars, muglike containers of a maize drink (*atole*) are lined up as well. This is a beautiful display of forms and colors. The Christian European breads of the kings are juxtaposed with the indigenous Mesoamerican tortillas and maize drink. Musicians play in the atrium and people gather there, going in and out of the parish church.

And now comes an important moment. The fiesta leader, standing in the atrium, calls out the names of the individuals who have been nominated or who have volunteered to serve for the coming year's fiesta. He asks the people of the community who are present and involved in the fiesta whether or not they agree that these men should be fiesta officials, whether they approve of these volunteers as being worthy of being officials. He addresses the community: "Do you agree?" (*¿Están de acuerdo?*), and people respond: "Yes, I agree" (*Si, estoy de acuerdo*). Sometimes some people disapprove, invoking reasons such as age or lack of financial means. The fiesta leader then welcomes the new officials and reminds them of the importance of fulfilling their duties for the patron saint fiesta.

In one such speech, in 1999, addressing the newly appointed fiesta officials, the fiesta leader reminded them of their ancestors who began this tradition, saying:

> God knows what sacrifices, what efforts our ancestors made, and what tears they shed, because those people really cried tears, to ask Our Lord His blessing and His aid, to help us in order to help in the creation of these duties that on this day we are still carrying on, in the steps of those who came before us.

> *Sabe Dios con qué sacrificio, con qué esfuerzo y con qué lágrimas, porque aquellos señores sí lloraban sus lágrimas, para pedirle a Nuestro Señor su bendición y su Socorro, para ayudarnos para que ayudaran a levantar estos cargos que ahoy estamos siguiendo todavía, estos pasos de aquellos antecedentes.*

Then the fiesta leader explained that Cruz del Palmar at the time of the ancestors was a little village already called Cruz del Palmar, and that now it is a little bit more "civilized." But he stressed that despite these changes,

We have to have faith in our traditions and bear in mind that if we are doing this, it is because we do it for the images inside our church, first Holy Burial, then Our Father Jesus and Our Lady of Sorrows. And in the name of all the blessed souls of purgatory who left their holy remembrance and indeed we remember them. They were humble and simple and had Christian faith. Because we are not doing anything except worshipping our patron saint, Holy Burial, patron of this community, Cruz del Palmar.

*Hay que tener fe en nuestras tradiciones y tenerlo en cuenta que, sí estamos haciendo esto, por intención a las imágenes que están ahí adentro de nuestro templo: el Santo Entierro primeramente, Nuestro Padre Jesús y la Virgen de los Dolores. Y a nombre de todas aquellas benditas ánimas del purgatorio, que nos dejaron su santo recuerdo, estamos recordando a través de este tiempo estos recuerdos. Y tan humildes y tan sencillos, y con aquella fe cristiana. Porque no estamos haciendo otra cosa que no sea en veneración a nuestro Patrón el Santo Entierro, de aquí de esta comunidad, Cruz del Palmar.*

The fiesta leader reaffirmed that the community would continue in the footsteps of the ancestors and maintain their traditions. In a rhetorical move aimed at involving his audience, he said again:

But in any case, not because it [Cruz del Palmar] is modernizing should we abandon our traditions. I think it is impossible, because there are memories that those who came before us left us.

*Pero de todas maneras, no porque se está civilizando, vamos a dejar nuestras tradiciones. Yo creo que no es posible, porque son unos recuerdos que aquellos antecedentes nos dejaron.*

Putting the question directly to the audience, he said:

Then, through what we are doing, because we remember, we will continue our traditions. Don't you agree? Yes or no.

*Entonces, a través de esto que estamos haciendo, de este recuerdo, vamos a seguir con nuestras tradiciones. ¿Qué dicen ustedes? ¿Sí o no?*

Then the fiesta leader led the audience in a prayer to Our Father (for excerpts of this speech in Spanish and English, see appendix C2).

After the fiesta leader reminds the new officials of their duties to the saint and the village, everyone present partakes in a ritual meal of broth, maize drink, and tortillas. The new officials receive the bread gathered in procession the night before and go into the church, where they kneel and are purified with this bread by another ritual leader of the fiesta. He ritually moves the bread in the four cardinal directions, making a figure that combines the Mesoamerican Four Winds ceremony and the Catholic sign of the cross. This counseling and blessing of the new officials lasts late into the night. When it is over, the newly inaugurated officials take their bread home to their families and soon, with their wives, return to the church, where a vigil is held with their participation (see appendix C4 for excerpts of speeches given during the vigil of the changing of duties). In the changing of duties, with its processions and ceremonies within them, every thing and every person has its place, its order, and its function, and this protocol ensures the continuity of the tradition from one year to another and from one generation to the next.

### Final Procession: January 7

January 7 is the final day and the culmination of the fiesta, and is a day of much exuberance. The crowd becomes enormous as visitors arrive from nearby towns and from as far away as Mexico City. All day long, especially in the afternoon, people gather in the parish church atrium. The French and the Apache dancers prance in the street in front of the atrium of the parish church, their usual space. The young rattle dancers dance, also in their usual spaces, within the atrium. The church bells ring loudly from time to time. Shortly after four o'clock the fiesta leader, his son, and a female ritual leader lead a procession out of the church atrium and through the town, followed by dancers, musicians, and many people. The female ritual leader rings her little bell. The procession stops at the cemetery, where the fiesta leader, his son, and the female ritual leader, along with a few others, enter. They quietly say prayers in front of an altar for the departed souls of the ancestors. When the officials come out of the cemetery, the dancers form two lines, thus establishing a path leading up the hill to the calvary. The procession goes through this path. Every single person enters the calvary, even the crazies, who have shown up too, dressed in their masks and costumes. Then the official of each dance group guides his group into the calvary. They enter in groups of four, and the fiesta leader and another ritual leader of the fiesta bless them. After everyone has been blessed, the long procession heads back to the church, and the calvary door is closed. During the afternoon there is much animation in that part of town, which is barren, rocky land and usually completely deserted. Many trucks and cars are parked, vendors sell food, and families gather and picnic.

The finale of the fiesta takes place in the atrium of the parish church. Guided by the fiesta leader, the procession coming from the calvary enters the atrium, where people move around in a circle while all the bands play in harmonious unison, quite different from the previous exuberant cacophonic minglings of different bands one could hear during the procession. Some dancers, mainly young children, as they move around throw peanuts, oranges, and other food at each other and at spectators. This is called the combat (combate). Then the people forming the circle in the atrium get down on their knees and go into the church. There they take part in a mass presided over by the priest of the town. Many of them are crying, because, as they say, they are happy and sad at the same time—happy that the fiesta was a success, sad that it is over, and perhaps sad because they might not be alive next year.

This is a moment of great emotional display. When the mass has concluded, all the bands in unison play two famous Mexican popular songs, "Good-bye Dear Mother" (*Adiós oh madre mía*) and "The Swallows" (*Las Golondrinas*). These are traditional Mexican songs typically sung for leave-taking, and are charged with meaning. *Adiós oh Madre mía* is a religious song sung to the Virgin Mary at the end of many celebrations. In *Las Golondrinas,* swallows depart, and their departure is sad because winter comes after they leave. This song is played when someone goes away on a trip, for instance at the airport or when somebody retires and leaves a place where he has worked for many years, and his friends hire a band to say good-bye. When a well-known artist or singer dies, *Las Golondrinas* may be played at his funeral (the texts of these two songs are in appendices C3 and C4). Toward the end of this event the children who danced in the atrium sit with their musicians and teacher and say good-bye in long emotional displays of appreciation. This whole event in the atrium is moving and intimate. It is a very touching and beautiful culmination to the fiesta during which a great feeling of togetherness and community pervades the place. People have come together one more year to participate in the fiesta, adore the saint, and partake in joyous and religious festivities together as a group, and they will gather again the following year.

## Masses

The Catholic priest of Cruz del Palmar also participates in ceremonies in honor of the patron saint, Holy Burial (Santo Entierro). The day of the saint, January 1, he presides over a high mass. And on the last day of the fiesta, January 7, he presides over a mass as part of the culminating ceremony. While the priest may officiate at several masses during the days of the fiesta, the January 1 mass is particularly salient. At noon on this day, church bells announce a mass, and all music, dancing, and noise stops. Outside, in the atrium of the parish church, mariachis play and sing religious songs, and the priest celebrates mass. Flowers and lit candles are on an altar erected in front of the church. People come from the entire village, as well as from nearby communities. The atrium is packed with people. In 1998 a delegation on horseback came for this particular mass from the nearby village of San Martin Caballero, carrying flags and the banner of Holy Burial of Cruz del Palmar. The delegation rode into town and right through the portals of the atrium of the church. The horsemen remained on horseback throughout the mass, with their hats respectfully off, held in such a way as to protect them from the sun. This was a particularly impressive ceremony which gathered these horsemen, with their finest attire, mounted on beautiful horses, standing in reverent formation in front of the parish church.

On the day of the saint, everyone goes to church—the mass takes precedence over all other activities. Mariachis from the region, on several occasions in which we participated, in front of the altar constructed in the atrium, in impressive full and spectacular attire, began the ceremony with the playing and singing of a repertoire of religious songs. In 2001 the mariachis seemed to be particularly affluent, given the quality and elegance of their costumes. The mariachi music was followed by a sermon by the bishop from the city of Celaya and some words from the local priest. The priest praised the faithful; the bishop talked about the evils of the world and the church's position on them. The priest and the bishop represent official, hierarchical religion, which is most prominent at the mass. At the same time, the adorned panels decorated and erected in front of the church and in the atrium and the decorated bread boards (*parandes*), also leaning against the church, represent popular and folk religious aspects of the fiesta.

## SAN LUIS DE LA PAZ/LA MISIÓN

Just as in Cruz del Palmar, in San Luis de la Paz, during the period of the fiesta, many processions, big and small, take place. These include a small procession to carry flowers to a house where a vigil will be held, the journey of the people from Cruz del Palmar to San Luis, and a series of processions between San Luis, San Ignacio, and La Misión, as well as an encounter in San Ignacio. Processions take place as well when saints go on visits (posadas) after August 25.

A very small procession before the fiesta occurs August 22. A group of men, women, and children take flowers to a house in La Misión, the Chichimec neighborhood outside San Luis, where a vigil will be held on August 23.

People remember that pilgrims from Cruz del Palmar came walking to San Luis de la Paz, as they say, "by land" (*por tierra*). For the people from Cruz del Palmar approaching San Luis, their logical last stop, given the layout of the land, was at a chapel called San Nicolás, where the couple who lived there would welcome the pilgrims and fed them. The following day they would continue their journey. Now both communities make the trip by small truck or bus, and on August 23 or 24 the delegation from Cruz del Palmar sleeps in the chapel of San Ignacio.

On August 24, the day before the official day of the fiesta, a procession in San Luis de la Paz leaves from the house of the first fiesta leader of the board of Holy Burial toward the chapel of San Ignacio, a neighborhood within San Luis, for an encounter with the people who have come from Cruz del Palmar. At the head of the procession is the first fiesta leader. He is followed by the bearers of two flags, the Mexican flag and a blue flag, a transformation of the French flag, used by a dance group from one of the neighborhoods of San Luis de la Paz. Then come the dancers from La Misión, followed by a row of people carrying saints, two Holy Burials in the middle of the row, each flanked by a statue of Saint Louis and statues of the medical saints Cosmé and Damian. Two female ritual assistants from La Misión participate as well. This procession is joined by another group from another neighborhood that carries another Saint Louis and an adorned panel (here called a chimal). Stick rockets are exploded in the air. When the conjoint procession arrives at San Ignacio, bells chime loudly, and the fiesta leaders of Cruz del Palmar and the female ritual assistant wait in a line with their saints.

The encounter in San Ignacio is quite similar to that which takes place in Cruz del Palmar. The leaders of each group kneel in front of the other and perfume the other group's saints with resin. The saints are lined up in a row and people kiss each one, crossing themselves each time. When the people of

San Luis and from Cruz del Palmar have finished this ceremonial encounter, a procession forms and goes to the church of San Luisito in the center of San Luis de la Paz to leave some of the saints there, then proceeds to the chapel in La Misión, where an adorned panel is being woven outside.

On August 25, the day of Saint Louis, an enormous procession takes place. It begins in La Misión and includes La Misión's French and Apache dance group with its musicians and people and officials from La Misión, as well as the visitors from Cruz del Palmar. Along the way the procession stops at some of the houses of the slaves, who kiss the saints. Their houses are adorned with red and royal blue paper, the colors of the French flag and Saint Louis. It is remarkable that the participants in the fiesta, instead of hating the French, their enemies, actually love them, because Saint Louis is their patron saint. In a way, the French are identified with Spaniards, and in another sense they are the compatriots of the saint. As this procession makes its way to San Luis it is joined by processions coming from some twenty neighborhoods of the town, each with its music, dancers, saints, and officials. Many different groups of French and Apache dancers, each with different costumes, as well as many plumed dancers walk and dance in this procession (see description in chapter five). Those who are not from La Misión wear expensive outfits, some very much like cowboys and cowgirls. The participation of girls is fairly new, a local reflection of a Western cultural phenomenon introduced by films and rodeos. There are no crazies, but there is some cross-gender dressing. In this procession men also carry an adorned panel. The very long procession goes down to the town square and circles around it. Then it proceeds to the church of San Luisito, where a priest and two altar boys welcome it and then head it up, thus taking it over at the church. Saint Louis is returned to the church and the adorned panel is erected in front of it. During these events the church bells chime and dancers dance. This procession, lasting several hours, is a huge event full of exuberance and dynamism. It is remarkable for the number of dance groups, consisting of children and adults of all ages, the lavishness of their costumes, and their evident enjoyment in participating in the honoring of their saint.

In the days following August 25, in San Luis and the Chichimec neighborhood of La Misión, very small processions go from visit to visit. People begin by sharing food, singing, and praying in the house where the visit is being held, in honor of the saints. After this is finished the participants take the saints out of the house and form a procession. People carrying flowers lead the procession, along with a female ritual leader or other older woman carrying a resin burner and red flag and ringing a little bell. Sometimes, on arriving at the next house, women change the clothing of Saint Louis. He may now wear a new dress, in white silk, with gold decorations, an offering from one of the participants. This is probably the result of a promise (*manda*) from one of the participants. In San Luis de la Paz, as distinct from Cruz del Palmar, the saint is never taken to a calvary or the cemetery.

The processions of Cruz del Palmar and San Luis de la Paz, and especially the encounters between the two groups, are felt by some participants, in particular teachers and other intellectuals, to be reenactments of the peace treaty between the previously warring Chichimecs and Otomis. The encounters between the two communities, Cruz del Palmar and San Luis de la Paz, are one of the highlights of the two fiestas and their linkage.

Considerable planning and preparation are involved, and the result is a great sense of pageantry. The music, bells, dance, flowers, and stick rockets all contribute to this intersection of official and popular religion, of indigenous and Catholic influences, of solemn, boisterous, joyous, serious, and playful behavior. Devotion and energy emanate from these processions. The ritual leaders, specialists, and assistants carry out their tasks with fervor. The musicians perform with gusto. The dance groups parade proudly in full array. The people who accompany the processions display commitment and happiness. The many onlookers are interested and curious. They show respect: some cross themselves, some men take off their hats. Processions, encounters, ceremonies, and masses are ways in which the community expresses devotion to the saints.

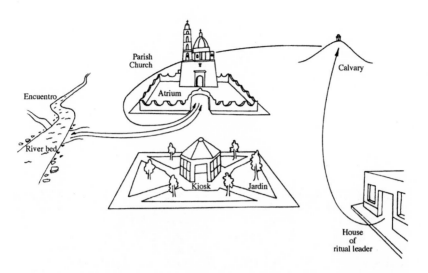

FIGURE 4.1

*Cruz del Palmar procession itinerary. Drawing by Fernando Botas.*

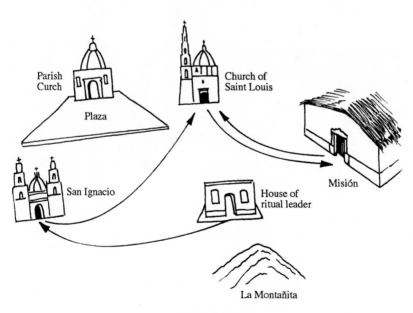

FIGURE 4.2

*San Luis de la Paz procession itinerary. Drawing by Fernando Botas.*

FIGURE 4.3
*Fiesta officials at head of procession in Cruz del Palmar. Photograph by Joel Sherzer.*

FIGURE 4.4

*Fiesta officials at head of procession in San Luis de la Paz. Photograph by Yolanda Lastra.*

FIGURE 4.5
*Fiesta officials at head of procession in San Miguel de Allende. Photograph by Joel Sherzer.*

FIGURE 4.6
*Arrival of people from Cruz del Palmar to join people from San Luis de la Paz in the encounter outside Cruz del Palmar. Photograph by Joel Sherzer.*

FIGURE 4.7
*Ritual greeting during encounter in Cruz del Palmar. Photograph by Joel Sherzer.*

FIGURE 4.8
*Procession from La Misión to San Luis de la Paz. Photograph by Yolanda Lastra.*

FIGURE 4.9
*Women carrying flowers and children in the procession in Cruz del Palmar.*
*Photograph by Joel Sherzer.*

FIGURE 4.10
*Bread carried in the procession of the gathering of breads (*recojida de panes*)
in Cruz del Palmar. Photograph by Joel Sherzer.*

FIGURE 4.11
*Rattle dancers* (danzantes de sonaja) *in Cruz del Palmar procession.*
*Photograph by Joel Sherzer.*

FIGURE 4.12
*French and Apache dancers in procession in San Luis de la Paz.*
*Photograph by Yolanda Lastra.*

**FIGURE 4.13**

*Promenade of the cow (*paseo de la vaca*) in Cruz del Palmar. Photograph by Joel Sherzer.*

# DANCES, DANCE DRAMAS, AND ENTERTAINMENTS

From the time of the arrival of the Spaniards to the present day, observers have been fascinated and impressed by the spectacular dances and dance dramas of Mexico. The Aztecs had elaborate dances, and the Spaniards introduced the dances of the Moors and Christians (Moros y Cristianos) to convert the natives and to celebrate this conversion. Today, performances of dances and dance dramas are major moments in patron saint fiestas.

The same dance groups that participate in processions also perform on their own. Rattle dancers (danzantes de sonaja), young girls and boys, shake tin rattles (sonajas) as they dance, adding still another element to the sound-scape of the fiesta. If there are several groups, as is usually the case, each group is accompanied by a small ensemble of musicians—one trumpet, one saxophone, and two violins. They play short, catchy, melodious tunes in a major key, constantly repeated, with the string and the wind instruments alternating. The children perform figure dances derived from French court dances. They move in various formations, creating oblong figures, each in front of or next to an adorned panel (crucero), often in the atrium of a church. When they parade in processions, they perform the same figures. They take their task seriously, with order and discipline.

In front of a church or on a square adjacent to it, French and Apache (Franceses y Apaches) or French and Chichimec (Franceses y Chichimecas) dance groups, opposing Europeans and Indians, stage constant skirmishes. These two opposing groups fight with real machetes or wooden sticks and are accompanied by loud drumming. In some places, for example Cruz del Palmar, these battles are choreographed into full-blown dance dramas during which French soldiers and fierce Indians engage in mock battles or create figures to the rhythm of music. Characters dressed as Death, the Devil, and Monkey are part of the spectacle. They play tricks on dancers and bystanders. Indeed, this is truly total theater. Some rather extraordinary events take place, with astonishing outcomes.[1] These dance dramas are called by some scholars *danzas de conquista*. It is intriguing that such dances take place in twenty-first-century Mexico (the implications are discussed in chapter six).

Very popular and spectacular plumed dancers (*danzantes de pluma, concheros*) offer imagined renderings of Aztec dancers and dances. One or several dancers play drums and an armadillo shell (concha) with strings, similar to a lute. An important aspect of the music is the tinkling of the small bells (*cascabeles*) worn on the dancers' ankles. Men, women, and children line up in military formation and perform stylized energetic figures. These groups are associations of individuals who want to recreate a mystic Aztec past, with its spirituality and rituals.[2]

Crazies (locos), accompanied by a powerfully amplified sound system, dance the meringue and other popular contemporary Latin dance forms in wildly exaggerated fashion, with no overt choreography or special spatial arrangement. In Mardi Gras style, these rowdy groups often give candy and beads to children.

Men and cardboard and wooden bulls perform mock bullfights accompanied by musicians playing a violin, trumpet, and a little drum during the dance of the bulls (baile de los toritos). This dance takes place either in front of a church, or in a square, or during processions. Giant puppets (mojigangas) also perform, accompanied by a loud brass band. They make odd movements as they sway back and forth, gesturing provocatively.

Dances and dance dramas last for hours and can take place several days in a row. All that was noted previously for the dances of the conquest—the agility and physical strength of the dancers, the rhythmic quality to the gestures, the kinesics, the music—is true for all fiesta dances, in varying degrees. Young boys and girls, adolescents, and adult men and women all participate.[3]

Dancers often perform because they promised their saint they would or they asked him for favors. "I have a cold, but I dance for my saint" (*Soy resfriado, pero le bailo a mi santo*), a boy told us. An official from San Luis de la Paz explained that he had to dance because "the dance, like the Chichimec language, is my race" (*la danza como la lengua chichimeca es mi raza*). However boisterous or bawdy the dances might be, the dancers are deeply religious, and that is why they dance. At various moments during the patron saint fiesta they enter the church and pay homage to the saints, kneeling and crossing themselves.

Groups of dancers often come from and typically are invited from different communities or neighborhoods within a town. They belong to associations (*cuadros*) whose members dedicate themselves to the dance, including taking care of the choreography, costumes, music, and rehearsals. A fiesta official in charge of the dance in a particular community may be the one who directs an association or who invites a dance group. Larger, wealthier, and more traditional communities invite more groups.

From a young age, children are socialized into the dance groups. It is quite moving to observe a man or woman dressed as an Apache or a plumed dancer dancing along with a young son or daughter wearing the same costume. When the children get tired the parents pick them up and carry them, all the while dancing, or they stop at a stand for food or drink and a rest. Sometimes entire families come together as crazies, wearing the same or related disguises. Several generations are involved. Since people dance for many hours, just as during processions, helpers offer water and juice to the dancers. Dances and dance dramas during fiestas are spectacles that mobilize a great number of people and talents in exuberant displays of costumes, colors, noises, energy, and music.

In addition to observing these various dances, people in the community go to public dances that begin in the evening and last till dawn. They feature well-known bands that play Norteño music, attracting huge crowds. In some places in the region, for example the Valle de Maiz neighborhood of San Miguel de Allende, *huapango* groups are also very popular, and people dance all night long to them. People delight in huapangos because they involve lively dancing, improvised verses of a cutting political nature, biting satire, comedy, and poetry. Rodeos, theatrical and musical performances, competitive contests, and spectacular fireworks entertain people during patron saint fiestas as well. Posters in front of churches, in stores, and on poles announce these events in the community and in adjacent villages and towns.

From late at night to early in the morning, the communities celebrating their patron saint stage elaborate pyrotechnics. Spectacular fireworks light up the sky. Typical Mexican devices are always part of the fiesta. The castles (castillos) that burn, indeed explode, are intricate structures made of bamboo and wire to which are attached fireworks and stick rockets. As they burn, they make complex designs that disappear quickly. They are costly and spectacular affairs. The other typically Mexican objects are the little bulls (toritos) also made of bamboo and wire. Men run with them around the square chasing children. The little bulls eventually burn up after having made a lot of noise. Huge stick rockets (cohetones) that sound like cannons explode in cascades of fire. The patron saint fiesta requires an excess of fireworks, and people evidently take pride in being able to offer these to the saint and to the community.

The fiesta may also be an opportunity to have a rodeo (jaripeo) or a horse race (carrera de caballos). These events are a reflection and expression of this cattle- and horse-raising region. Another activity is called the gathering of chickens (junta de pollos), during which people go from house to house accompanied by musicians and beg for chickens, which will be distributed to members of the community who have distinguished themselves through their participation in the fiesta.[4]

The fiesta is also an occasion to erect a greased pole (palo ensebado), with hanging prizes such as clothing, food, and other items, in front of the church on the square. Young boys and men climb it individually or in groups, trying to get to the top. Their first task is to somehow scrape off the thick layer of grease from the pole with their legs and hands as they hoist themselves up. Greased pigs are released to be caught by daring young men. Some fiestas feature all-night theatrical performances (coloquios) that retell the story of the birth of Christ. Musical interludes, dance performances, and clownish skits, as well as the recitation of poetic and deeply religious verses, characterize these events. People come from all over to watch the plays that take place in May during the fiesta of the Holy Cross in Valle del Maiz, a neighborhood of San Miguel de Allende.[5]

Children are not forgotten during patron saint fiestas. Fiestas are the occasion of a family outing during which parents bring their children to ride merry-go-rounds and play games. Fiestas are also a time for shopping at the numerous stalls erected in front of every store, in every corner available. If street eating is popular in Mexico, it is magnified during fiestas. Visitors clearly take pleasure in eating the food served during these events. "In the countryside during fiestas one eats real Mexican food" (En los ranchos durante las fiestas se come comida mexicana auténtica), a visitor from Mexico City commented. The food that can be purchased at the stalls includes beef barbeque, tacos, tostadas, corn on the cob, fried pork rind (chicharrón) with sauces and spices, pickled pig's feet, and cotton candy. The food displays, the merchandise sold, the colorful balloons and toys for children, the picturesque merry-go-rounds, and the decoration of the houses and in the streets confer aesthetic qualities on the fiestas.

### CRUZ DEL PALMAR

During the long, multiday fiesta in Cruz del Palmar, many of the dances and entertainments mentioned here occur. The parish church, the atrium of the church, and the square in front of the church are the center of these activities. They include the rattle dance every day of the fiesta; the French and Apache dance drama on January 1, the day of the patron saint; the dance of the crazies on January 1 and again on January 7, the final day of the fiesta; the dance of the enormous puppets on January 6, the evening of the changing of duties (cambio de cargos); and the public dance in the evening of January 1. A brass band plays in the bandstand in the center of the square (jardín) on January 1, and mariachis play at the mass on January 1. A rodeo (jaripeo) attracts ranchers and visitors from the region on January 5. Climbing a greased pole takes place on January 5, and fireworks and the burning of the wooden castles and bulls liven up the central square on January 1 and January 6, the evening of the changing of duties.

## Rattle (Sonaja) Dances

Throughout the fiesta of Cruz del Palmar, three groups of young boys and girls, about twenty in each group, dance in the atrium of the parish church, each at the foot of an adorned panel (crucero) with which they are associated. The adorned panel of the Holy Burial of the Center (Santo Entierro del Centro) stands on the left side of the entrance to the church and the adorned panel of Our Father Jesus (Nuestro Padre Jesús) stands on the right. The adorned panel called Our Lady of Sorrows (Nuestra Señora de los Dolores) stands in front of the little calvary at the entrance to the atrium. One group of dancers and musicians is from Cruz del Palmar, the other two groups come from nearby villages. One of the violinists is the teacher with whom the group learned the steps and practiced. From the day permission to hold the fiesta is granted, at the end of November, rehearsals for the dances have taken place, organized by the official in charge. They rehearse every day for a month. The fiesta official is obliged to provide meals for all of them.

The three groups dance all day long, every day, til dark, during the entire fiesta, and their music is ever-present. They are interrupted only by pauses for meals. These dances constitute a well-organized event whose purpose is to honor the saints. It is lovely and touching to see groups of children wearing flowered hats and shaking rattles, dancing for the patron saint of their community.

## Dance of the French and Apaches

January 1 is a day of much excitement and exuberance in Cruz del Palmar. People arrive throughout the day from neighboring towns and further away, including the Mexican capital, Mexico City, and the United States. They come in cars, on horses, and on foot. Some of the visitors carry and use cameras and video cameras. The streets of the village are decorated, with banners and paper cutouts (papel picado) of various colors. Food and drink stands, amusement rides and games, and a market selling kitchen utensils, clothing, and other items are set up in the streets around the church. People eat, drink, and visit. Many people dress up for the event. A festive atmosphere prevails throughout the town.

All morning long, in the street in front of the church atrium, the French and Apache dancers prance about, in figures and mock combat, a precursor of the dance drama that is to take place in the afternoon. The music of the young children's rattle dance groups can be heard coming from the atrium, along with several other bands playing loud music.

At noon, church bells announce the mass, and all music and dancing in the town stops. The priest presides over the high mass in the atrium of the church. The mass ends with the priest announcing to the packed atrium, "Now begin your fiesta" (*Ahora empiecen su fiesta*). And the dance between the French and the Apaches, the Cruz del Palmar version of the dance between Europeans and Indians, begins. The Apaches, also called the striped ones (*rayados*), wear white pants and yellow tunics with horizontal rows of dangling pieces of tin; hence the term *rayados*. Their faces are painted with black-and-white patterns deliberately made to look wild. On their heads they wear a white feather headdress. The French wear blue pants and shirts and a red kepi, reminiscent of contemporary French policemen's hats, from which hangs a white cape, sometimes decorated with a cross or the inscription "*Fransia*."[6] Both groups are armed with wooden machetes or sticks. Some Apache may carry a bow and arrow. The French carry a French flag and the Apaches a Mexican one, with the Virgin of Guadalupe replacing the eagle. Death, two Monkeys, and the Devil take part in the dance. Death is dressed in white from head to foot. On his head, which is completely hidden, he wears a silver crown. He carries a wooden scythe with a red wooden blade. Monkeys are dressed in gray, wear masks on their faces, have tails, and carry whips. The Devil has a white suit and wears a red mask with a white beard and moustache.

Unlike on other days of the fiesta, when they merely prance or create patterns during the procession, on January 1 the French and the Apaches participate in a choreographed dance drama. This drama stages battles between the Apaches and the French, which the French always win. The French and the Apaches line up on opposite sides of the street facing one another. The Apaches are adjacent to the atrium of the parish church and the French on the other side of the street. The four musicians, two of whom play big drums and two others violins, line up behind the French. They accompany the dance rhythm, and also lead it. The music is lively and frenetic; it punctuates and galvanizes the fighting. The sound of the wooden sticks striking each other during the skirmishes is part of the aural experience.

Each side consists of twenty young boys and occasionally a girl, about three to fifteen years old, sometimes older. The two sides fight an endless series of stylized battles as in a Zorro film, one on one, beginning with the oldest of the soldiers on each side and ending with the youngest and smallest, who, immersed in their task, diligently follow the story and choreography just as the older dancers do. The French win every single individual battle, and it is Death, the Monkeys, and the Devil that finish off each victim. In the words of one of the dancers, "The Indian dies, the French win, and Death, the Devil, and the Monkey kill" (*El meco muere, el francés gana, la muerte, el diablo, y el chango matan*). Amazingly, despite the fierce fighting of the Apaches, the French win all the time. As humorous and as playful as this fighting is, it nevertheless evokes the skirmishes, battles, and terrible massacres that took place during the conquest.

When each Indian falls to the ground, Death, with the aid of the Monkeys, mimes opening his stomach, pulling out his entrails, humorously called tripe stew (*menudo*) by onlookers, and eating them, in an obvious reference to human sacrifice and anthropophagy. There is even a red dye on the ground simulating blood. Each scene may be longer or shorter, more or less humorous, but basically, Death cuts the slain Indian into four parts, then Death and the Monkeys eat the entrails. The number four, a symbolically magic number in Mesoamerica, appears at various moments of the fiesta, including the very important Four Winds ceremony (see chapter six).

The drama is full of humor and satire. Death occasionally goes after audience members and mimes cutting them with his wooden scythe, causing much laughter, a humorous reminder that we will all die one day. From time to time an audience member, perhaps an ex-dancer, enters the dancing and fighting for a few minutes. The Monkeys grab the sexual parts of the dead Frenchmen. This all goes on in a playful, parodic way. A large audience of old and young, coming and going, stand around the dancers in the hot sun, talking, eating, and drinking as they watch the unfolding drama acted by their children, brothers, sisters, and friends. They enjoy the story, as well as the ways in which Death, the Devil, and the Monkeys play eagerly and with gusto with the dancers and members of the audience. The dancers' behaviors are bellicose and humorous, wild, unruly, and ferocious. After the last Apache is killed the dancers dance to a different step, putting themselves in a squatting position, and then they all go have lunch, including the ones who were killed.

## Other Dances

On January 1, simultaneous with the French and Apache dance drama being performed in front of the parish church and the rattle dance going on inside the atrium, in one corner of the square a group of crazies dance boisterously and erotically to salsa, merengue, and rock music blasting from a sound system. Their outrageous masks and costumes, their blasting world beat music, and their provocative movements all draw attention to them. The crazies return to Cruz del Palmar on January 7, the last day of the fiesta, when they participate in the culminating procession. Giant puppets appeared on the evening of January 6, 2001, the night of the changing of duties (cambio de cargos). We are not sure whether they will remain a regular feature of this fiesta as they are elsewhere in the region.

## Other Entertainments

In addition to the various activities and performances we have just described, the dances, dance dramas, crazies, and giant puppets, on January 1 a lively brass band plays polkas and waltzes in the bandstand in the square in front of the church, families sit on benches and eat and shop at the various stands, and children ride the merry-go-rounds. On January 5, men erect a greased pole that attracts daring adolescents to earn its prizes: toilet paper, diapers, toys, tequila, kitchen utensils, and other items. In a field at the entrance to the village on the same day a large dug-out space transformed into a bullring is the site of a rodeo, and many people from nearby villages come on horseback to compete. On two different nights, January 1 and January 6, the square is lit up with spectacular fireworks, burning castles and little bulls.

## Public Dance (Baile)

On January 1, from early in the evening until dawn, in a large outdoor grassy area one block away from the central square in front of the parish church where other activities, including fireworks, are taking place, several bands play music and people dance. This dance is advertised by means of posters in San Miguel de Allende, San Luis de la Paz, and elsewhere. The crowd is large and consists of local individuals as well as people from other communities. There is an entry fee, and beverages, including beer, can be purchased. The air is electric with excitement before the music begins. People of all ages dance until dawn.

The music ranges from norteño music, played by small groups and most appreciated by older people, to well-known groups, bandas, that play a more globalized music, often with a techno beat, which younger people like best. There is thus a crescendo in order of bands, from small to large, from simple to complex, from traditional norteño to techno. The latest group is the loudest and the most electrified, and technologically the most sophisticated. It is the best known and attracts the most people.

From nine o'clock on, traditional Mexican fireworks, the burning of several wooden castles, take place in the square in front of the church. The simultaneity of events adds to the excitement of the totality. Like the rest of the fiesta, this music, the dancing, and the clothing worn by the people, their hats and their boots, are all an expression of the traditions and identities of the region. The bands are often chosen and financed by individuals working in the United States. Cruz del Palmar, ordinarily a quiet ranching community, becomes a crowded, dynamic, exuberant place during its fiesta.

## SAN LUIS DE LA PAZ

The events that take place in San Luis de la Paz during its patron saint fiesta are configured somewhat differently from those at Cruz del Palmar. Compared with Cruz del Palmar, San Luis de la Paz is a big bustling town, and its patron saint fiesta is a celebration shared by the indigenous Chichimec population of the neighborhood of La Misión with the many other neighborhoods of the town. In conjunction with the fiesta, the chamber of commerce and various associations sponsor a regional fair with cultural, agricultural, commercial, and livestock exhibits. Rodeos and carnival rides are part of the fair. Food stands are to be found everywhere in the streets.

### Dances

The dances in San Luis de la Paz, while massive and involving many groups, are limited to two types, the French and Apache dances and the plumed dances. The rattle dance, the crazies, and the giant puppets are not present, although they may be introduced in the future. On August 24, the day before the official day of the fiesta, French and Apache dancers and plumed dancers from La Misión and other San Luis neighborhoods dance in La Misión in a large space. They arrive in a procession and leave in a procession, forming figures and patterns. One year a newly created plumed dance group from Cruz del Palmar participated in the fiesta. It had been formed by a ritual leader, who, with the assistance of government financing, designed and made the costumes with his wife and choreographed the steps. He was the musician, clad in white, playing the mandolin and dancing. The dancers wore blue velvet dresses with golden decoration, feather headdress, and anklets made of small bells. Compared with groups from other neighborhoods, the group of French and Apaches from La Misión, because of lack of money, often has simple costumes. The French wear khaki pants with blue stripes down the side and a white shirt. They carry machetes, and one carries a blue flag. The Apaches are bare-breasted and wear a loincloth and anklets with small bells. One of them carries the Mexican flag.

On August 25, a festive mood pervades the neighborhoods of San Luis de la Paz. Many decorations, including ribbons, hang from churches and houses. They are blue, the color of Saint Louis. In late morning the priest officiates at a mass at the San Luis Rey parish church. The French and Apaches from La Misión are joined by some twenty groups of other French and Apache and plumed dancers, and each of the groups in turn performs in the small, intimate square in front of the church of San Luisito where a beautiful adorned panel has been erected. This panel, constructed in La Misión, is an offering from the Chichimecs to Saint Louis. The French and Apaches dance, prance, and fight but do not perform a dance drama as they do in Cruz del Palmar and some other places. They get involved in impressive skirmishes with machetes. They are excellent fencers with machetes. The sounds of their drums and of metal clashing fill the little square. Both parties remain standing and dancing. It is a dance of skirmishes that nobody wins (for an interpretation of this stalemate, see chapter six).

Bystanders look pleased and excited while watching the variety of costumes worn by the many dance groups coming from the different neighborhoods of the town. The French and Apaches might wear gray, red, black, or beige pants or skirts with golden stripes on the sides, blue scarves, and cowboy hats. The French definitely look European, wearing simple clothes and manifesting a military bearing. In contrast, the Apaches wear spectacular outfits. Bare-breasted and in loincloths, they exhibit their vigorous and muscular bodies. They wear huge, multicolored plumed headdresses. Some have silver ornaments and yellow fringes on their loincloths; some wear leggings or anklets made of bells. Some carry shields with arrows. They could not look more like the stereotype of the savage Indian.

Many groups of plumed dancers, with their stringed armadillo shell (concha) or drums, parade in spectacular formations of men, women, and children. All the members of a group wear the same costume, huge feather headdresses, loincloths, pectoral ornaments, and anklets with bells. They execute dance patterns to the rhythm of their music. Their dancing is very different from European dance forms. They are frequently called Aztecs (Aztecas). They consciously want to recreate what they imagine to be prehispanic Aztec dances. Exuberance and excitement characterize this extraordinary spectacle of all the groups, who perform proudly and with brio, representing their communities and honoring their saint.

## Other Entertainments

On August 24, in La Misión, stands sell food such as tostadas and beverages such as *pulque colanche,* a very strong fermented traditional drink made from the red tuna fruit. On both August 24 and 25, in the various neighborhoods of San Luis de la Paz, food and drink are sold. Outside of town one finds a fair (*feria*) with Ferris wheels, merry-go-rounds, shooting galleries, games of various kinds, and food and drink stalls. In a prosperous town the size of San Luis de la Paz, rodeos and bullfights are an important part of the fiesta.

Like all of the activities of the patron saint fiesta, the dances and other entertainments in Cruz del Palmar, San Luis de la Paz, and the region around them are a mixture of the religious and the profane, sometimes solemn but usually boisterous. They involve various and overlapping musical performances, a profusion of events, and the massive enjoyment of people of the communities and visitors. They reflect and express much of Mexican folklore and Mexican display and panache.

The elaborate dances, dance dramas, and other entertainments give rise to many questions. What is the relationship between the dances and the popular religion practiced in the area, in particular the cult of the saints? How can we interpret the French winning over the Apaches in the dance dramas in Cruz del Palmar, while in San Luis de La Paz the skirmishes between the two end in a draw with no victor? What do these dances and dance dramas express, represent, and symbolize? These and many other questions are explored in the next chapter.

FIGURE 5.1
*Rattle dancing in atrium of Parish Church in Cruz del Palmar.*
*Drawing by Fernando Botas.*

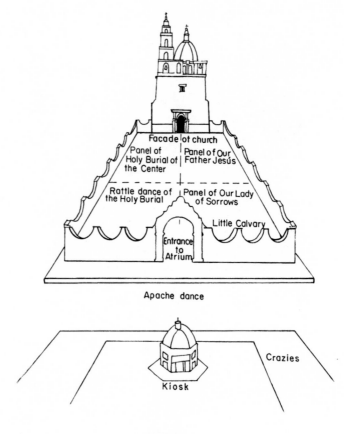

Facade of church

Panel of Holy Burial of the Center | Panel of Our Father Jesús

Rattle dance of the Holy Burial | Panel of Our Lady of Sorrows

Little Calvary

Entrance to Atrium

Apache dance

Crazies

Kiosk

FIGURE 5.2
*Location of adorned panels and rattle dances in Cruz del Palmar.*
*Drawing by Fernando Botas.*

FIGURE 5.3
*Dancing in front of San Luisito Church in San Luis de la Paz. Drawing by Fernando Botas.*

FIGURE 5.4
*French and Apache dancers in Cruz del Palmar. Photograph by Joel Sherzer.*

FIGURE 5.5
*Battle between French and Apache dancers in Cruz del Palmar.*
*Photograph by Yolanda Lastra.*

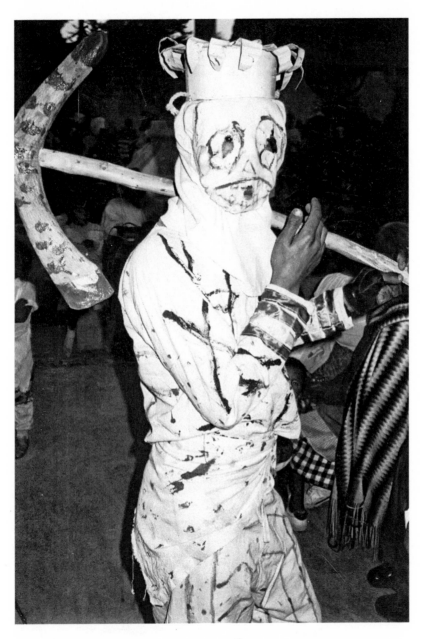

FIGURE 5.6
*Death dancer in Cruz del Palmar. Photograph by Joel Sherzer.*

FIGURE 5.7
*French dancer in Cruz del Palmar. Photograph by Yolanda Lastra.*

FIGURE 5.8
*Rattle dance in Cruz del Palmar. Photograph by Yolanda Lastra.*

FIGURE 5.9
*French dancers in San Luis de la Paz. Photograph by Yolanda Lastra.*

FIGURE 5.10
*Plumed dancers (*danzantes de pluma/concheros*) in San Miguel de Allende.*
*Photograph by Joel Sherzer.*

FIGURE 5.11
*Crazies (*locos*) in Cruz del Palmar. Photograph by Yolanda Lastra.*

FIGURE 5.12
*Crazies (*locos*) in Cruz del Palmar. Photograph by Joel Sherzer.*

FIGURE 5.13
*Giant puppets (*mojigangas*) in San Miguel de Allende. Photograph by Joel Sherzer.*

# SIX

# TOWARD UNDERSTANDING THE
# PATRON SAINT FIESTA

What do patron saint fiestas signify for the communities and the people who participate in them? What do these fiestas reveal about their cultural behaviors and practices? What is the significance of the various dances and processions that take place during fiestas? What is the significance of the religious practices associated with patron saint fiestas? What aesthetic principles organize the fiestas? Is there a continuity in tradition? What is permanent, what is changing? Why? What do these vigils, processions, encounters, ceremonies, and dances tell us about people's identity? Activities, participants, spaces, topography, sounds, music, costumes, and food all have deep symbolic meanings and significance. In this chapter we offer some interpretations of the events and practices associated with patron saint fiestas.

## SIGNIFICANCE OF THE PATRON SAINT FIESTA

The patron saint fiestas of Cruz del Palmar and San Luis de la Paz, as well as patron saint fiestas in general, are extremely important moments in the lives of these places and their inhabitants. The fiestas are thought of, imagined, constructed, invented, prepared for, and indeed lived for throughout the year. They mark both the time of year and the passing of another year. They link the past, the present, and the future. As Ingham has written, "Their focus on popular religion constitutes a system of signification through which social order is experienced, communicated and reproduced."[1] Their existence and recurrence make them part of the specificity of the place and identity of the people.

The patron saint fiesta is a time for pleasure, eating, drinking, dancing, and praying. It provides an aesthetic enjoyment through an abundance of ceremonies, music, and processions. During the exuberant days of the fiesta the community, the people, and especially their saints are on display. In the words of a famous huapango player, the fiesta is an expression of the magic and the traditions of Mexico (*"Mexico es magia y tradición"*).[2] The patron saint fiesta is a performative event that produces temporalities, sacred spaces, actors, and stories to remember.[3]

The patron saint fiesta also reaffirms family ties. Husbands and wives collaborate, as do children. Fiestas are an expression of the beautiful tradition of the Mexican family. Parents show their deep love for their children in the way they dress their children for the occasion and actively involve them in the fiesta. Children are well behaved and serious about their tasks. Relatives who have migrated to other parts of the region or of Mexico or to the United States come back and take part in the celebration of the saint and in praying for the family's ancestors' souls (ánimas). The event reinforces peoples' sense of community. The organization of these elaborate fiestas implies a community and groups of people, young and old, who can help each other, work together within families, villages and towns, and the region, and who can draw on resources that individuals in other parts of Mexico or immigrants in the United States can contribute. It is striking that all the events of the patron saint fiesta are group activities that require collaboration. Musicians come in groups of various sizes, depending on the activity; dancers perform in groups; vigils are attended by twenty to thirty persons, as are ritual meals; and processions bring together hundreds of people. Men making an adorned panel and altarpiece work in groups of two or three or more. Several women—grandmothers, mothers, daughters, and other women of the family or the neighborhood—work together in the kitchen. Each individual in a community is part of a group that honors the same saint. Every year the collaboration necessary for the complex organization of the fiesta reaffirms its social and ritual structure, organized by the fiesta leader and fiesta officials. And, of course, what is significant about the fiestas of Cruz del Palmar and San Luis de la Paz is their special ritual and historical linkage, the encounters within and across them that originally brought them together, which is expressed each year during their fiestas.

These networks of relationships are effective because of ethical principles that govern the behavior of the inhabitants of the communities. They feel a sense of duty, expressed by the verb *cumplir,* which means to fulfill one's duty, to carry out one's promise. *Cumplir* is a verb participants in the fiesta use when asked about the fiesta. It is related to a set of other notions—obligation (*obligación*), promise (*compromiso*), and compliance (*conformidad*). One must carry out one's promise to the saints, to one's family and friends, to fiesta officials, and to the fiesta itself. *Cumplir* has personal, social, and religious meanings. It is because so many people work together, are faithful to their promise, and perform their duties that the immense investment in time and money make the patron saint fiesta possible each year.

The necessity of reciprocating is part of this system. If Cruz del Palmar invites a musician from San Miguel de Allende to perform in a vigil, later on someone from Cruz del Palmar will go help him during a vigil. The visitors from San Luis de la Paz are guests of the people of Cruz del Palmar during the fiesta for Holy Burial, and those of Cruz del Palmar are the guests of the people of San Luis de la Paz for the fiesta of Saint Louis. Of course, we did hear of cases in which reciprocity was not honored, which meant that the relationship between the two parties was broken. And there are rivalries, jealousies, rancor, and hereditary feuds between individuals, as well as disputes over costumes, roles, places, and shrines. Observers might be surprised by the rowdiness, drunken disorderliness, and abusive clowning that can occur during a procession, in the waning hours of a vigil, during meals, or between events, but somehow the rowdiness is held in check by and subordinated to the deep religiosity and orderliness pervading all phases of the fiesta.[4]

A striking feature of the patron saint fiestas we observed in villages or small towns, and in Cruz del Palmar and San Luis de la Paz in particular, was the sociability and the conviviality that permeated every moment of the multiday event as a result of the common effort to honor the saint. Hospitality is an important feature highly valued by the people. After a meal in honor of the people of San Luis de la Paz who were leaving to go back home, a ritual leader from Cruz del Palmar delivered a leave-taking speech (*despedida*) using a set of formulaic sentences enjoining God to protect the visitors:

> May God help you, open the gate for you
> Open your heart, your goodness, your charity
> That you may not lack money
> That you may have goods, charity;
> That the Lord in heaven, owner of hearts,
> Of goodness bestow on you good luck, good fortune.

> *Dios te socorra, te abra la puerta*
> *Que te abra el corazón, tu bien, tu caridad*
> *Que no falte el dinero*
> *Que abunden tus bienes, tu caridad;*
> *El Dios de los cielos quien es dueño del corazón*
> *Del bien [te conceda] una buena suerte, una buena fortuna.*

On another such occasion a fiesta leader opened his farewell speech by saying, "I feel sorry because I have not taken good care of you" (*Me siento yo apenado no los he atendido muy bien*). People feel it is a duty to treat their guests well. These practices were also extended to us. One aspect of sociability that is prevalent during fiestas is the cultural theme of accompanying (*acompañar*), that is, of being with, sharing the moment with, friends, actual and ritual kin (*compadres*) and the saint.

Sharing of food is ever-present during fiestas. This practice has been referred to as collective commensuality (*commensalidad colectivas*).[5] Many activities of the fiestas are events during which food is served and consumed as a group. People eat together during vigils, and dancers eat together between performances. In Cruz del Palmar the whole village shares food during the changing of duties. Hospitality and conviviality are also present in all households. The fiesta is a time when families get together. Children, relatives, and friends come from far away, and huge groups of people share meals and living quarters in the houses of the village or town. In public places, on squares, and on street corners, food stands are erected everywhere and stay open late into the night. People eat in the open, by themselves or with their family and friends. The fiesta is a time for hospitality, generosity, and abundance during which people are united or reunited.

Various types of verbal interaction also display the sociability that is one of the hallmarks of patron saint fiestas. Individuals greet each other with respect; they display politeness and reverence and perform ritual embraces. Sometimes people express special affection. This is illustrated in speeches in which religious leaders address the audience as "dear ritual friends" (*compadritos*), using the suffix -*ito* as a form of endearment. Asking permission (*pedir permiso*) of God, the saint, and the priest is a form of respect. People often use the expression, "if God grants us permission" (*si Dios nos da licencia*). Walking in processions with other people to accompany the saint (*accompañar el santo*) also shows respect and devotion.

But the fiesta is also a time for talking and joking, moments of togetherness, sharing humor, making fun in a good spirit, and eliciting laughter. Ritual leaders are masters of ceremonies who greet and welcome visitors from elsewhere with speeches and bid them farewell when they leave. After vigils or ritual meals they might also address the people present. In Cruz del Palmar, during the changing of duties the ritual leader addresses the whole village. These moments highlight the unity of the people present. The speech delivered by a religious leader from Cruz del Palmar at a ritual meal in San Luis de la Paz reiterated the traditional honoring of the saints and reinforced the links between the two communities. Such speeches insist on the culture the participants share and on the significance of the fiesta, expressed in their own language. A sense of *communitas* and intimacy pervades the atmosphere at such events, as it ultimately does throughout the fiesta.[6] Here is a portion of this speech (more of this speech is in appendix D):

> He is God, Compadre Félix, Comadre Remedios, Comadrita Lola, and the rest of the community who come from Cruz del Palmar. . . . Well, let us hope in God that the blessed souls, and all the saints, and those who left us these traditions and these devotions will help and bless us wherever we may be, that they will open the doors for us, that we will not lack our daily bread.

> *El es Dios, Compadre Félix, Compadre Remedios, la Comadrita Lola, y demás comunidades que vienen de la Cruz del Palmar. . . . Pues, esperemos en Dios que las benditas ánimas, todos los santos, y aquellos que nos dejaron estas tradiciones y estas devociones, que nos socorran que nos bendizcan donde quiera que estemos, que nos abran nuestras puertas, que no nos falte nuestro pan de cada día.*

## PATRON SAINT FIESTAS AND DANCES

The dances and dance dramas performed during patron saint fiestas offer a complex of intersecting meanings that need to be unpacked. In the words of Sylvia Rodríguez, they "involve symbolic processes that metaphorically express, encode, and enact information about social and ecological relations, as well as about major forces that shape group history."[7] What ideas, metaphors, allusions, and historical references are expressed in the dances and dance dramas of Cruz del Palmar and San Luis de la Paz, and more generally in dances in the region?

Let us return to the questions posed in chapter five. The dances enact bellicose encounters, skirmishes and battles, between Europeans and indigenous groups. Undoubtedly these fights replay, consciously or unconsciously, what happened during the conquest. Do they express the trauma sustained by the ancestors of the present-day individuals at the hands of the Spaniards? Certainly. However, the favorable view held by the practitioners of the cult of the saints of their own conversion is noteworthy. For instance, Christopher Columbus is honored in the region. His statue stands prominently on a street corner in the center of San Miguel de Allende. He is praised in songs sung at vigils as the bringer of Christianity. Instead of being a conquistador who opened the door to massive killing and oppression, he is viewed as a benefactor.

Why Apaches in the middle of Central Mexico, in particular Cruz del Palmar and San Luis de la Paz in the twenty-first century? In the mid-nineteenth century, the Apaches living in northern Mexico were fought by the Mexican army. Apaches were the fiercest Indians known to the people of this region. They were striking in appearance on their horses, with head-dresses, war paint, and weapons. They have come to represent the epitome of the Indian savage as pictured in books and Westerns, as well as in the dances and dance dramas of patron saint fiestas in Central Mexico.[8]

Why French soldiers? The French are part of nineteenth-century Mexican history, when Maximilian and the French occupiers tried to conquer and rule Mexico. French invaders under Maximilian were defeated by the Mexicans in the battle of Puebla on May 5, 1862, leading to the Mexican national holiday, *el cinco de mayo,* and this event might have been taken into consideration by the choreographers of the dance. Despite the Mexican victory at Puebla, the French later gained control of Mexico City and established a French-supported government there. It was not until 1866 and 1867 that the French troops were withdrawn. Apparently, while in the region near San Miguel de Allende, French soldiers, as a goodwill gesture, participated in dances performed by Chichimecs. Perhaps for this reason the dances since then have characters disguised as French soldiers.[9] The dance drama of the French and Apaches stages a war or series of battles between indigenous natives and European invaders. Key to the possible multiple references and interpretations of the French and Apache dance drama and its relationship to the patron saint fiesta is the fact that the foreigners defeated the Indians, yet the Indians survived despite everything. Dances are also reminders of the cruelty and brutality of the sixteenth-century conquest.

Why this type of dance, and not other European dances? The most common dance drama performed in Mexican fiestas, as well as elsewhere in Latin America, is the dance of the Moors and the Christians (Moros y Cristianos), also known as the dance of the conquest (danza de conquista), which was introduced by the Spaniards. Dramatized battles between Moors and Christians have been documented in Spain as far back as 1150.[10] After 1492, to celebrate victory over the Moors and to convert them, spectacular dance dramas were produced in Spain. Priests acted in these dance dramas and in them converted and baptized the Moors. The spectacle included enormous fireworks and boats on the water. The Spaniards brought and adapted these dance dramas to the New World as a means of converting the Indians.[11] The

Central Mexican dance drama of the French and Apaches is, then, this region's version of the Moors and Christians dance.

According to this interpretation, the French represent the Christians, that is, the Spaniards who fought and defeated the Moors and expelled them from Spain in 1492, and the Apaches represent the Indians conquered by the Spaniards. The French are symbolic transformations of the Christians and the Apaches are symbolic transformations of the Moors. The French win because they are Europeans, agents of the conversion of the Indians to Christianity. For the people of this region, this dance, and indeed the entire fiesta, is a reaffirmation of their conversion and ongoing faith, symbolized at the end of the fiesta of Cruz del Palmar, on the last day, in the final procession, by one of the Indians carrying a cross.[12] Relevant here as well is that many of the ballads (alabanzas) sung during vigils praise and celebrate the conversion of Indians to Christianity. When we asked one of the officials in Cruz del Palmar why the Indians die in the drama, he answered, "Yes, they die, but we are here" (*Sí, ellos mueren pero nosotros estamos aquí*), meaning "we (are) Indians (and) are still here." The conquest of Mexico is not yet complete.

In Cruz del Palmar and other places, an intriguing behavior during the mock battles between the French and the Apaches is the French eating of the Indians' entrails. History and stereotype have it that Mesoamerican Indians sacrificed the vanquished and offered their hearts to their gods. The Spaniards considered this practice a sign of the savagery of the Indians and used it as one of the arguments put forth to convert them to Christianity. In the drama enacted today, the French eating of the entrails of the Indians is an ironic symbolic inversion, quite humorous and greatly appreciated by the audience. This event can be interpreted as a subversive and powerfully meaningful action, an underlying and perhaps unconscious expression of knowledge that the conquerors—the Spaniards—were brutal and cruel invaders.

In San Luis de la Paz, the French and Apaches engage in lively skirmishes. The French fight valiantly and the Indians fiercely defend themselves, uttering stereotypic Indian war cries. But no winner or loser emerges; rather, the outcome is a dynamic status quo. The French and the Indians coexist, expressing metaphorically the co-presence of the two traditions, the European—the Spanish—and the pre-Columbian Chichimecs, in San Luis de la Paz. This Indo-Hispanic mixture is also the ethnic and racial makeup and the cultural identity of the members of the community. This is true both of the patron saint fiestas we studied and of the region more generally.

The plumed dancers (danza de pluma, concheros) floutingly affirm their pre-Columbian roots. These dances are from Otomi origin but are imagined to be Aztec because of the constructed prestige of the Aztec empire.[13] They are often called concheros, because several dancers play the armadillo shell (concha). By dancing in front of the church on the day of the patron saint, the plumed dancers continue a tradition of indigenous dances that already existed. They affirm their double identity and implicitly state, "We are Indians and we are Christian."

A type of crazies, men dressed as women, existed in pre-Columbian times and were adapted immediately after the conquest as characters to mock the Spaniards. Ancient masks worn by crazies can be found in antique stores in the region. Today, groups of crazies who take part in patron saint fiestas continue this tradition of satire and now mock Mexican history, current Mexican, American, or international politics, and U.S.-Mexican relations. Similarly, the giant puppets of Spanish origin are humorous and satirical representations.

The crazies and the giant puppets are two of the bawdiest, most grotesque, and satirical components of the patron saint fiesta and might be interpreted as mocking and desacralizing Christianity. But these humorous, bawdy, grotesque, and satirical behaviors are typically carnivalesque. They began in Europe in the Middle Ages and were tolerated and indeed encouraged by the Church, to enable letting off steam. These behaviors were also practiced in indigenous communities. And in both communities, in the past and in the present, there was and probably still is a counterhegemonic undercurrent.[14] And yet the crazies, like the French and the Apaches and the plumed dancers, also enter the church and the calvary and honor the saint, thus showing their devotion to religion and religion's ultimate control over them. As we were told by participants, "the crazies dance for the saint" (*los locos bailan para la imagen*). Coupled with rowdiness, an expression of devout adherence to Christianity creates a tension that is an important dynamic component of these fiestas.

The dance of the rattles in Cruz del Palmar and other neighboring communities is European in style of music and dancing. It expresses no sarcasm, no satire, no counterhegemonic hint. Yet it is a reminder of the European takeover of the native culture. At the same time, the groups dance in front of adorned panels, indigenous artifacts, thus expressing the juxtaposition of the European and indigenous cultures.

Dances and dance dramas honor the patron saint, but they also replay history, enable the affirmation of identities, and recognize the positive and the negative influence of the conquest. They are also sources of creativity, humor, and satire.

## PATRON SAINT FIESTAS AND RELIGION

The extreme devotion of the practitioners of popular religion in Cruz del Palmar, San Luis de la Paz, and the surrounding region is remarkable. Opening the festivities for the fiesta of Santa Cruz in the Valle de Maiz neighborhood of San Miguel de Allende, the famous Central Mexican huapango performer Guillermo Velázquez Benavides declared, "This festival is not for tourists; it is for us, for our soul, for our saint" (*Esta fiesta no es para turistas; es para nosotros, para nuestra alma, nuestro santo*).[15] This statement, which elicited thunderous applause, certainly applies to the patron saint fiestas of Cruz del Palmar and San Luis de la Paz. Mr. Benavides has been coming to and performing at the Valle de Maiz fiesta for eighteen years and feels it is his duty to come. This duty clearly motivates all practitioners of the cult of the saints.

Understanding the patron saint fiestas of Cruz del Palmar and San Luis de la Paz requires placing them in the context of the long tradition of devout religiosity of the area. This can be followed from pre-Columbian times, to conquest and conversion, through the mid-twentieth century Cristero revolt against the postrevolution Mexican state, to contemporary practices such as the erection of home altars and the placing of representations of saints in public places such as markets and bus stations. The people of this region are extremely devout and, of course, Catholic. Talk to any bus or taxi driver, passengers on a bus, sellers in markets, maids, manual workers, or immigrant workers living in the United States and they will tell you about their patron saint fiesta and often that of nearby places, describe to you what happens during the fiesta, and explain the meaning of such practices as limpias and Cuatro Vientos and such objects as copal, crucero, and ramillette.

While not necessarily in opposition to or in conflict with the official church, the patron saint fiesta is much more a practice of the poor and the indigenous, that is, of "deep Mexico," even though in poor urban neighborhoods and in rural villages and towns the same populations are practitioners of both the official church religion and popular religion. Thus, both the official Catholic Church and popular religion honor crosses and saints, Christ, and the Virgin Mary, but each does so in its own way and with different emphases. The official church has a hierarchy, from the pope to cardinals and bishops to priests, along with monasteries and orders, monks and nuns. It is male dominated and dogmatic. There is little place for women.

The social organization of popular religion is the civil-religious fiesta official system, locally organized within villages and towns. It is much more egalitarian in orientation, including with regard to gender, than the official church. And while churches are loci of religious activity in both official and popular religion, what happens in each is different. Popular religion makes use of a broad array of other sacred spaces as well, including home altars, rooms in private houses, fields, squares, streets, calvaries, and cemeteries. And many religious objects and practices are unique to popular religion, in particular fiestas, including adorned panels, altarpieces, red flags, resin burners, ritual encounters between places, endless processions, all-night vigils, dance dramas, music and dance performances, and the use of various plants in rituals. The cult of the saints in fiestas, the centerpiece of popular religion, represents a system of holiness and power without the intercession of priests, an autonomy and independence outside the official church.[16]

Rather than being in conflict or opposition, the official Catholic religion and the popular religion of this area, the cult of the saints in fiestas, are two religious expressions that intersect and overlap in various ways and constitute a continuum along many dimensions. There is no denying a certain tension between the official church and popular religion. Each side is suspicious of and critical of the other, yet each recognizes the need to cooperate. Many people are involved in both, and such practices as taking saints and other images in and out of churches and moving them about in processions are expressions of the intersection of these two faces of Mexican Catholicism.

This raises a set of puzzling questions with regard to the relationship between the official church and popular religion, in particular its manifestation in its most important moment, a patron saint fiesta: Who is challenging whom? Who is resisting whom? Is the official Catholic Church the hegemonic master, both religiously and politically, that is being resisted by and subverted by popular religious practices?[17] Or is popular religion really in charge of people's hearts and minds, beliefs and practices, and resisted by the obviously more powerful (in the nation-state and the world) Catholic Church? Who conquered whom? Did Spanish Catholicism conquer indigenous religion or did indigenous religion conquer Spanish Catholicism?

The official church hierarchy, along with the middle and upper classes of Mexico, often categorizes popular patron saint fiestas as superstitions and black magic practices that resist and subvert the dominant order and "proper" religion. The practitioners of the cult of the saints, on the other hand, consider adoring their saints a duty that was transmitted to them by their ancestors, who embraced the Catholic faith. They feel they have been blessed by this beautiful faith. They reiterate the necessity of honoring the saints in their own way in speeches, songs, dances, and processions, despite the frequent objections and opposition of the local priests.

So, there is resistance on both sides. Both the official Catholic Church and popular religion challenge, resist, and invade the other. More important, however, each needs the other for its existence. While always resisting to a degree, challenging to a degree, and fighting to a degree, the official Catholic Church has permitted popular religion, in particular fiestas and the fiesta system, to continue to exist. Both official Catholicism and popular religion support one another because their base, the poor and indigenous of Mexico profundo, are believers in and practitioners of both. Popular religion is a religion of the Indian and the poor, whose fervent religious beliefs and practices are much more dominant and omnipresent in rural Mexico than religion as it is shaped and organized in the more secular, modern nation-state, especially Europe, the United States, and middle-class, urban Latin America.

Viewing patron saint fiestas as resistance only cannot account for the complexity of these events. Rather than focusing on resistance, we prefer a frame of reference that includes resistance as one of many dimensions, such as religious faith and fervor, the pleasure of honoring local saints, attachment to and returning to the rancho, getting together with family and friends, enjoyment of play, humor, music, dance, food, drink, and the general excitement of the fiesta, the recollection and acting out of historical events at a national and local level, and aesthetics, all of these creatively expressing, indeed affirming, identity.

## AESTHETICS OF PATRON SAINT FIESTAS

The celebration of the patron saint fiesta involves a very specific aesthetics. Particular textures, structures, organizations, performances, and symbolic and expressive forms necessitate creativity, craftsmanship, and traditions and they express the taste and pleasure of the people participating in the fiesta. The Bakhtinian notion of the carnivalesque, implying heterogeneity and multiplicity, best describes this type of aesthetics.[18]

Heterogeneity and multiplicity indeed organize the patron saint fiesta with its many performances, including vigils, processions, encounters, masses, dance dramas, rodeos, and ritual cleansings. Talk, jokes, prayers, songs, speeches, music, dance, fireworks, and food are elements and moments of these events. Heterogeneity and multiplicity are also at work in the extraordinary soundscape of the fiesta. Its mode is that of heterophony, that is, the co-presence of many different types of sounds in a single space. During processions, the music of each of the various dance groups, church bells, the little bell of the female ritual leader, and stick rockets, as well as other sounds and noises, can be heard. Loudness and lavishness are the desired effects.

Heterogeneity and multiplicity are present in all the details of the patron saint fiesta: in the rich, complex decorations of the altars, the profusion of flowers during masses and ceremonies, the composition of the processions, with the various dance groups and groups of musicians. Heterogeneity and multiplicity characterize the cultural thickness and density of the fiesta, in the sense that many layers of meaning, many allusions, and many references shape particular interactions and events.[19]

The heterogeneity of the fiesta is also brought about by a network of dimensions and oppositions that unfold into the structural flow of the fiesta. These include:

indigenous / Hispanic identity

Otomi and Chichimec (languages) / Spanish language

sacred / profane

tradition / change and innovation

day / night

sound / silence

talking / singing

sobriety / ritual inebriation

seriousness / ritual play and humor

inside / outside

life / death

harmony / disharmony

orderliness / disorderliness

control / boisterousness

The aesthetic characteristics of the patron saint fiesta confer on it a deep, complex, and constant coefficient of uncanny strangeness and weirdness, to borrow a phrase that has been used for the language of magic, perhaps not irrelevant here, since there is a magic, part actual, part metaphorical and symbolic, in the fiesta.[20] Many moments of the fiesta come to mind—Death and the Monkey eating the entrails of the Indians in the French and Apache dance drama and the audience calling it tripe stew (*menudo*); a ritual leader standing in the parish church and cleansing people with flowers or bread, or cleansing with a bottle of alcohol during a cleansing at a vigil; a group of Mariachis in full attire performing Las Mañanitas in front of the closed parish church at dawn with nobody around to hear, playing music for God and the saint; brass bands, which often purposely play out of tune[21]; the appearance of the crazies, transvestites strongly suggesting sexual transgressions, grotesquely and bawdily masked figures, here and there during the fiesta, from solemn and sacred occasions to profane ones, entering a parish church, a calvary, or a chapel; the constant contrasts of elements such as the grotesqueness of the crazies, the wildness and fierceness of the Indians, and the simple innocence and beauty of the little girls and boys with their hats adorned with paper flowers and ribbons, constantly dancing in front of a church; the ever-present interplay of sacred and profane—a poster of Mickey Mouse on the wall next to an altar in people's homes, alongside posters and pictures of the saints, Christ, and the Virgin of Guadalupe; alcohol and Coca-Cola on the altar next to images and statues of saints; the use of Apaches in dance dramas instead of local indigenous groups (Otomi or Chichimec) or the dominant indigenous group of Mesoamerica, the Aztecs. Similarly, there is a strangeness in the representation of history. Neither the medieval French who fought the Moors nor the French who fought the Mexicans in the nineteenth century had anything to do with the Indians. This dance drama in and of itself contains many uncanny, strange elements, including the fact that it is a celebration on the part of representatives of Mexico profundo of the defeat and conversion of their own ancestors, in a playful and mocking way.

Humor, like the uncanny and the strange, enters into the aesthetics of the fiesta. The bawdy behavior of the increasingly popular crazies is a good example. So is the playful way the French and Apaches, often acted by very young boys, fight endless battles with wooden swords in Cruz del Palmar and real machetes in San Luis de la Paz. Movingly humorous are the little boys and girls dressed as miniature replicas of their Apache father or plumed mother walking and dancing along with them. Very funny as well are the actions of Death and the Monkeys during the dance drama. Like the crazies, they can be bawdy. They also go in and out of their roles in the drama, chasing after audience members. The crazies, the giant puppets, and the stilt walkers grab people, touch them, and play with them. Humorous crazies stop in front of people with cameras and encourage them to take their picture; husbands often take pictures of their wives dancing with such crazies as Vicente Fox or other satirized political figures. People constantly laugh and joke, and all of this in no way conflicts with the overall religious frame of the fiesta. Enjoyment, in which play and humor are central elements, pervades the patron saint fiesta. Official religion is too dull, too tame, too controlled compared to this popular religion.

Humor and speech play are integral parts of the aesthetics of the patron saint fiesta. They occur during all aspects of fiestas, including the preparations for and breaks during ritual events, as well as in moments of eating, drinking, social dancing, and relaxing. A typical setting for humor and play is a gathering of men, come together to construct the adorned panels and altarpieces. Along with the eating of spicy food and the drinking of alcoholic beverages, there is much joking (*relajo*), that is, a typically popular Mexican combination of verbal dueling (*albures*), often loud, singsong intonation patterns, exaggerated facial and body movements, imitation of the speech of others, parody and comic routines, somewhat vulgar slang, feigned aggressive interactions and teasing, anecdotes and stories, jokes, complex puns and allusions to sexual matters, and laughter. There is also much joking about the food and drink, the spiciness of the former and the inebriation-producing effects of the latter, all alluding to sexuality and especially masculine sexual prowess. While this stylized and boisterous misbehavior with language is focused on masculine values and associated with men, women understand it and sometimes participate as well.[22]

Symbolic allusions can be complex. During a break in the singing of religious hymns during an all-night vigil as part of the fiesta of Cruz del Palmar, one of the young male musicians, quite drunk, looked at his mother, seated, wrapped in a serape, and sleeping, and said in Spanish, "She's like the smoking mountain." There was much laughter. The speaker was referring to the smoking volcano of Mexico, called by its Nahuatl name Popocatepetl, generally Popo, and alluding to the history and symbolism associated with Mexico's indigenous and ecological legacy, much a part of these people and this event. The mother is indeed like a volcano, powerful, protective, and explosive. Some moments before one of her grandsons had asked her permission to sleep on the woman's lap, and a few minutes later her drunken son suddenly went to sleep on her lap, then got up and began playing his guitar again. This woman and this set of events surrounding her are at the intersection of old and new, traditional and modern, serious and playful, which is so much what this fiesta is about.

A discussion of the aesthetics of the patron saint fiesta must include the hymns and ballads sung during vigils, with their special vocabulary, their religious and historical references, and their music (see chapter three). The speeches of fiesta leaders, officials, and ritual specialists, with their poetic and rhetorical features, are also expressions of the fiesta aesthetic.

The ritual objects, adorned panels and altarpieces built and woven for the fiesta, are artistic creations in their own right. Their creation requires knowledge of the plants and flowers used to make them and special craftsmanship to assemble them. The adorned panels standing in front of churches, decorated with desert palm and with many objects and food attached to them as well, again display this aesthetics of density and abundance. The altarpieces are the expression of a taste for balance and the harmonious combination of colors. These two creations, adorned panels and altarpieces, are mainly religious objects that need to be present during the fiesta but have now become collectors' items for some artists living in the area. The saints are often ancient statues of great value. They appear as little wooden figures delicately painted and adorned, with very expressive faces. They are dressed in lace or silk garments and rest, stand on, or are surrounded by small flowers or other decorations made of colored paper or beads. People venerate the replicas of their saints for their religious and symbolic significance. Other people adore them, too. Lately a number of them have disappeared and might end up in antique dealers' shops in the United States or Europe. The hanging in the streets of paper cutouts (*papel picado*), which are bright streaks of colors and lacelike patterns that stand out against the blue sky or dark night, is an example of the ephemeral art of the fiesta, which includes the profusion of flowers that fill the churches and the decorated breads, as well as the altarpieces and adorned panels.

Fiestas are a kaleidoscope of objects, patterns, movements, and bright colors that create an ephemeral, singular world, a special mood for a few days, which reoccurs from year to year. Each element, each moment, is exuberant in and of itself, and their coming together in a density of processions, dances, music, and ritual enactments is nothing short of spectacular and explosive. Mexican religious fiestas, in particular patron saint fiestas such as those in Cruz del Palmar and San Luis de la Paz, are so strikingly beautiful that they are the subject of photographic exhibits and essays.[23]

The amount of time, money, and work devoted to produce what is largely an ephemeral aesthetics is astounding, and all of it is for the saint, the community, and the participants. The aesthetics of patron saint fiestas are an excellent example of what has been called, in popular culture, "inwardly directed art"—art for the people themselves, not for collectors or economic gain.[24]

## INDO-HISPANIC CULTURE:
### TRADITION, CONTINUITY, AND CHANGE

The complexities of Mexican social, cultural, racial, and ethnic forms and processes have been debated by scholars, historians, anthropologists, and philosophers. They have coined a number of terms to talk about them. These terms include acculturation, syncretism, hybridity, and the Spanish word *mestizaje* (related to the ethnic social term *mestizo*).[25] In our opinion, none of these terms adequately captures what the patron saint fiesta represents, and we prefer the term Indo-Hispanic. Patron saint fiestas in Cruz del Palmar, San Luis de la Paz, and indeed all of Mexico are the product of this Indo-Hispanic world that emerged after the conquest.

We have described events, objects, practices, and performances with a profusion of detail. Now we want to discuss the possible or probable origins of various aspects of the fiestas, with the caution that while some of these are indisputable historical facts, agreed to by scholars, others are educated inter-pretations. What was already there in the indigenous world that made the Spanish cultural and religious conquest possible? What is the continuation of Spanish customs and practices? What is the continuation of indigenous customs and practices?

## Convergences of Indigenous and Hispanic Traditions

An observer noted as early as 1585 that Indians already had images of saints in their houses.[26] Little by little every city, every town, every village, and every neighborhood began celebrating its patron saint on the saint's day. When the two cultures came into contact, convergences and similarities enabled the development and acceptance of the saints and the creation of patron saint fiestas. It has been claimed that the dedication to saints is characteristic of communities that most preserved prehispanic beliefs.[27] As many scholars have remarked and as we have noted, acceptance of the Spanish religion was facili-tated by the presence of similar practices and beliefs in the native religions. Communities often chose saints with the same attributes as the native gods. The little mounds (cuicillos) that were places of worship used by the Indians often became the places where chapels were erected. When the Spaniards arrived, they were fascinated by the spectacular costumes, choreography, and movements of the Aztec dances and allowed them to be performed in front of churches.[28] When the Spaniards introduced their own dance dramas, the indigenous population accepted them.

The civil-religious hierarchy of offices (the carguero organization) that makes the enactment of fiestas possible in Mexico and throughout Meso-america had prehispanic roots as well as European. Mesoamerican glyphs and iconography portray the metaphorical notion of burden expressed in the Spanish term *cargo* and attest to the prehispanic existence of the system.[29] In the 1580s, Spanish authorities instituted the *cabildo* system, which gave some powers to Indians in matters of governance of villages and towns. The Span-iards also introduced guilds and confraternities, like the ones that existed in Spain, which enabled the natives to collaborate and work together. These two institutions played an active part in the organization of patron saint fiestas.[30] Today's system of organization of the fiestas, with leaders and officials, is a continuation of sixteenth-century practices. Our view is that there is a con-tinuity from both an indigenous form of social and ritual organization and Spanish social forms to the contemporary carguero system.

The Four Winds (Cuatro Vientos) ceremony performed during vigils and encounters and at various moments of the fiesta to purify the participants and the space where they gather is prehispanic, but it also corresponded to European beliefs. Scholars who have studied the chronicles and other docu-ments have been able to demonstrate that this kind of cross already existed in indigenous symbology and was linked to the four winds, which brought clouds and rain. This prehispanic cross was also the symbol of the four car-dinal points, the four stages of creation, the four basic colors, and the four vital elements, fire, water, air, and earth, which permitted harmony between humans and the cosmos.[31] The Franciscan and Dominican friars were con-vinced that the four winds were the four elements discussed in European antiquity.

Encounters (encuentros) in fiestas, in addition to having probable indige-nous roots, may be related to Christ's encounter with his mother on the way to Calvary; the same word, *encounter,* is used. This is dramatically enacted in San Miguel de Allende during Holy Week. In Spain there are encounters of different saints with Christ in processions. Other elements of contemporary fiestas that occurred in both the Old World and the New include greased poles and the use of drums.

Monkeys, who are humorous actors in French and Apache dances and dance dramas and comic actors in processions, can also be traced to both European and prehispanic cultures. Monkeys have appeared in European paintings since the Middle Ages. They appear as jugglers or peasants, and more generally are part of the European artistic expression of the grotesque. In the words of Serge Gruzinski, "The figure of the monkey is loaded with symbolic meaning, and its exotic nature places it naturally next to strange and fantastic animals."[32] At the same time, "These animals [Monkeys] occupied a special place in ancient Mexico. The Indians fed them without difficulty and were amused by their predilection for women. . . . They were represented as thoughtful and human like. They were equally present in myths and rituals. . . . The Nahuatl [speakers] associated the monkey (*ozomatli*) with good for-tune, joy, and with a negative sense, libertine life."[33] Monkeys are widespread in myth, ritual, and ecology in prehispanic Central and South America, often involved in the kinds of humorous antics Sahagún reported in Mexico and that contemporary monkey figures reproduce in the French and Apache conquest and conversion dances, as well as in processions. Still other cultural features found in both Spanish and indigenous expressive cultures that are present in patron saint fiestas include men dressed as women, devils, crazies, giants, death, and loud noise.[34]

In addition to these accidental convergences, several practices and objects are the result of conscious mingling of prehispanic and Hispanic elements. The dances opposing Europeans and Indians derive from both Moors and Christians and Indian dances.[35] The five-stringed armadillo shell (concha) is a prehispanic, regional animal shell with European strings, with the result that the performer produces European melodies such as those that might be played on a guitar or mandolin. Ballads sung during the vigil combine European strophic structure and voice tense typical of indigenous singing.

## Spanish Traditions

Some practices that were introduced by the Spaniards in the sixteenth century are still present today in the region and are part of the patron saint fiestas. The organization of space in communities is still the one created by Spanish friars according to the Hispanic design and conception of cities and villages. The central plaza with the church, schools, and streets is the space of today's fiestas.[36] The Spaniards also introduced cattle and horses into the region and developed a cattle culture with ranches.[37] The rodeos that take place during the fiestas, the promenade and slaughtering of the cow, and the serving of broth made from the cow are Spanish customs still practiced in Spain.[38]

Sometimes fiesta leaders and officials (mayordomos, cargueros) use military titles such as as *capitán* and *sargento* to refer to themselves. This reflects Spanish influence. The existence of associations, confraternities, slaves, and boards (esclavos, mesas) that take care of the saints is also Spanish. The fiestas for patron saints involve processions, music, church bells, and fireworks, as they were practiced in Spain. In the 1550s, the Spanish Church hierarchy ordered that processions be accompanied by music to increase the devotion of people and incite them to attend services. And music and banners had to be part of patron saint fiestas.[39] These practices, introduced by the friars who came to New Spain, are still present today in patron saint fiestas in Central Mexico.

The dance dramas of French and Apaches display features found in dances of the Moors and Christians performed in Spain since the Middle Ages. Like the Spanish dances, they are part of religious celebrations that glorify a saint. They stage battles, they are dramatizations of real situations, and they are celebrations of faith.[40] We might consider that the altarpiece (ramillete) used during the fiesta is modeled on the Catholic monstrance, introduced by the Spaniards. Its etymology, "little bunch," is Spanish. The string instruments found in several musical groups were not prevalent before the conquest and are of Spanish origin. The flute (chirimia), of Asian origin, was introduced by the Spaniards. Stick rockets, church bells, and the little bell rung by the female ritual leader are of Spanish origin. The little bell is rung at the most solemn moments, as in Spain and the rest of Catholic Europe, at the time of elevation of the eucharist at mass.

### Indigenous Traditions

Indigenous practices are also still apparent in fiestas. Cleansing (limpia) was pre-Columbian, often conceived of as sweeping and purification, and was and still is performed with various objects, including candles, perfumed smoke, flowers, bread, and paper figures.[41] The perfuming of the saint with resin (copal) continues a pre-Columbian Mesoamerican practice. Copal (a word of Nahuatl origin) was considered the incense of the gods. The tradition of flower and song (flor y canto), an Aztec poetic-metaphorical couplet meaning "poetry," described eloquently by Fray Diego Durán in the sixteenth century, has remained alive. Much music and song and many plants and flowers embellish patron saint fiestas today. In particular, desert spoon (cucharilla), already mentioned by Durán, is still used in the construction of adorned panels and altarpieces, ritually intrinsic objects in the fiesta.[42] People in the community we talked to interpreted the adorned panel, present in all the patron saint fiestas of the region, as either a bed or a stretcher used for the wounded in warfare or as a battle shield, as one of the words for it, chimal, of Nahuatl origin, would indicate. Another possible origin is a palanquin used to carry Mesoamerican god images and divine rulers. Evidence for this is again the glyphs and iconography.[43] The Historia Tolteca Chichimeca refers to an offering to God in the form of a stretcher to which a man was tied, then killed by a multitude of arrows.[44]

The word tenancha, which we translate as "female ritual leader," is of Nahuatl origin (te-nan-tzin = one's dear mother), and this female ritual official appears widely in Mesoamerica. The role, which gives a woman an important place in the celebration of the saint, is an expression of Otomi culture, which gives initiatives to women. Asking permission of the supernatural and rendering public counsel to the new fiesta officials by village or community leaders are still practiced in indigenous communities in Central and South America.[45] The belief in the existence of a spirit world and its importance for the living is of prehispanic origin and remains widespread today.

The Mesoamerican acknowledgment of death is present in many moments of the fiesta, as exemplified by the figure of death in the French and Apache dance drama and the procession to the cemetery, the constant invoking of departed souls, and frequent reminders of mortality. The number four, significant in Mesoamerican religious practice, is present in the fiesta, especially in the Four Winds ceremony and in the cutting of defeated Indians into four parts during the French and Apache dance drama. People enter the calvary on the hill in Cruz del Palmar on the last day of the fiesta to be blessed in groups of four.

The food consumed during fiestas consists of the Mesoamerican subsistence crops, beans, squash, and chili, eaten with maize, in solid or liquid form, as in prehispanic times. Tobacco was used ritually by indigenous groups, and its ritual use continues today. People are offered cigarettes at vigils. Ritual joking and humor, an important element in fiestas, are widespread in Mesoamerica and have indigenous roots.[46] Until recently the languages of the fiestas in Cruz del Palmar and La Misión neighborhood of San Luis de la Paz were Otomi and Chichimec, respectively. Now the language used, primarily but not exclusively, is Spanish. Indigenous discourse practices, however, such as ritual greetings and leave-takings, conversational interaction, and public counsels, are part of the fiesta, as are verbal styles such as repetition and parallelism, used in formal speeches.

A notable feature of the fiesta organization, and probably a remnant of the initiatives taken by indigenous people, is the existence of itinerant ritual leaders and officials. These individuals are well-known in the region. They travel or are invited from place to place to officiate at an all-night vigil, to play music and/or dance at a fiesta, or generally to perform a ritual role. The groups of musicians that perform in processions, in front of churches, or in the main square of a town during patron saint fiestas are also itinerant and, like the ritual leaders, go back to the mid-sixteenth century. After 1560 the Spanish clergy, alarmed by the beauty and sensuality of religious ceremonies, forbade the teaching of music in churches and monasteries and the organization of lavish fiestas. However, Indians in towns and villages continued to celebrate their patron saint fiestas and needed music. Unemployed native singers and musicians previously attached to churches and monasteries began forming itinerant groups that traveled about from place to place, and this custom is still ongoing.[47]

The complexity of the history of these communities, which appears in all of the manifestations of the patron saint fiesta, reflects both pre-Columbian cultural forms and practices and colonial Spanish cultural domination. Patron saint fiestas are the result of interactions, imbrications, and transformations, due to convergences and juxtapositions of customs, attractions, and impositions since the sixteenth century.[48]

## From the Past to the Present

Patron saint fiestas have been taking place since the sixteenth century. As early as 1585, images of saints and groups dedicated to the cult of saints were created, and they continue to this day. The attachment to the saints that began then is due to the energy, strength, and power attributed to them. Dances of conversion found all over Latin America began soon after the conquest. The dances in Cruz del Palmar and San Luis de la Paz, as well as the hymns and ballads sung during vigils, are examples of the representation of the conquest through expressive culture, which appeared as well in Nahuatl codices and texts.[49]

Documents and studies from the early part of the twentieth century describe activities that we have observed in Cruz del Palmar, San Luis de la Paz, and other communities in the region between 1997 and 2006 and attest to the continuity and vitality of these patron saint fiestas. In 1933 young men were inspired by a picture of an Athapaskan Indian to create their Apache costumes.[50] In 1943 Frances Gillmor noted the discordant kinds of music mixing together and the crowding of influences, Aztec, European, religious, and secular, creating confusion and togetherness.[51] In 1947 Frances Toor described the abundant fireworks and reported the existence of night vigils during which people sang hymns and ballads, performed the Four Winds ceremony, and made and blessed altarpieces. She also noted during fiestas the eating of traditional Mesoamerican food, corn, beans, squash and tortillas, prepared as before the conquest, and the ritual drinking of alcoholic beverages and the serving of cigarettes, offered to human and spiritual participants.[52]

Reporting on his fieldwork in the 1950s, what Eric Wolf said of the relationship among religion, fiestas, and aesthetics is quite relevant to our approach here:

The religious complex also has aesthetic functions. The *fiesta,* with its processions, burning incense, fireworks, crowds, color, is not merely a mechanism of prestige and of economic justice. It is also "a work of art," the creation of a magic moment in mythological time, in which men and women transcend the realities of everyday life in their entry and procession through the magical space of the vaulted, incense-filled church, let their souls soar on the temporary trajectory of a rocket, or wash away pains of life in holy-day drunkenness.[53]

In 1966, Robert Ricard described the cult of village patron saints in fiestas, processions, dancing, and singing, all part of what he called "the spiritual conquest of Mexico."[54] Gertrude Prokosch Kurath in 1967, reporting on her earlier research, listed the basic elements of Central Mexican fiestas that we still find today, such as dances and dance dramas, the singing of hymns and ballads, processions, and the Four Winds ceremony. She argued that participants in these events were in search of Indian traditions and that the expressive forms were a mixture of indigenous and European. She posited that their music used European harmonies and Indian rhythms.[55] In 1978 a guide to fiestas in Mexico offered a long yet incomplete listing and a short description of fiestas throughout Mexico, including Central Mexico. Among the events described were giant puppets, rodeos, dances, and processions.[56]

The current fiesta leaders of Cruz del Palmar and San Luis de la Paz, now in their fifties, remember their parents and grandparents taking part in the fiestas for Holy Burial and Saint Louis, and express the opinion that these fiestas have been taking place since the sixteenth century. In 1998 a 103-year-old woman from San Luis de la Paz, who died five years ago, told us that as a young child she was carried to the patron saint fiesta of Cruz del Palmar by her grandfather, who began the pilgrimage to Cruz del Palmar in 1872. She said, "I was raised in this devotion" (*Yo en esta devoción me he criado*). She remembered they carried a banner, dating from 1880, and took along figurines of Holy Burial (Santo Entierrito) and Saint Louis (San Luisito). She named the places they stopped along the way, where people offered the pilgrims beans and tortillas. A ritual leader from Cruz del Palmar, now seventy-five years old, told us he had been going to San Luis de la Paz for sixty years.

Tensions are also part of the tradition of the patron saint fiesta. Spain brought the saints and the dances, and Spanish authorities wanted to have control and impose their views. They were leery of too much independence and too much initiative on the part of the Indians. The practice of the fiesta since the beginning of the conquest has been a source of both conflicts and negotiations with the official church, and this adversarial posture continues today. The parish priests are often at odds with the fiesta leaders. They accuse the leaders of paganism and idolatry, and hint at black magic. In San Luis de la Paz a few years ago the local paper reported that people refused to let the statue of San Luisito be moved from its original, traditional place in the church of San Luisito to the parish church. Consequently the priest refused to hold mass in San Luisito. In Cruz del Palmar, the priest refused to let the people take the little statue of Holy Burial for the fiesta. So it remains in the church, and the people use the little saint that belongs to San Luis de la Paz instead. However, people in the communities constantly work to maintain their traditions as they want them to be and modify them as they deem appropriate, not as the priests or the higher church authorities wish. Several scholars have documented the hostile behaviors of priests and other church officials.[57]

Tensions can exist as well within the community. People have different opinions with regard to the choreography of dance dramas. The placement of people in processions may be a very delicate matter, and because this has to do with questions of visibility, rank, and prestige, rivalries emerge. In one of the communities we studied someone mentioned to us that "the fiesta leader is very lazy, but we help him" (*el mayordomo es muy flojito pero lo ayudamos*). Tensions always existed and no doubt will continue to exist; people accommodate to them.

Even though Mexican patron saint fiestas are an expression of deep Mexico, of the ancient, indigenous past of Mexico, they are not relics, museum pieces, or frozen in time and space—quite the contrary. Fiestas such as those of Cruz del Palmar and San Luis de la Paz are dynamic, ongoing, and constantly creating and inventing themselves in new and fascinating directions, all the while maintaining a tradition that goes back five hundred years or more. The interplay of tradition, continuity, and change can be seen in all aspects of the fiestas of Cruz del Palmar and San Luis de la Paz, which are constantly adapting and remaking themselves. The encounter, which originally was a procession from one town to another, has now become part bus or truck trip, part walking pilgrimage, as the participants from the visiting location arrive in a bus or truck at the outskirts of the location they are visiting and then walk the rest of the way in a procession.

Participants now carry digital cameras and video cameras, recording their own fiesta, and thus are becoming more and more observers as well as participants, and thus more and more apt to discuss patron saint fiestas in an informed way. In fact, each fiesta is a commentary on previous fiestas as well as on fiestas to come. Migrants who contribute work, money, and influences from elsewhere make the fiestas more elaborate and lavish.

Dance and music in particular are sites of change and adaptation, innovation, and creativity. While the dances performed by young boys and girls are relatively stable from year to year and place to place, they vary in participation. In some years and at some places, the dancers are all young; at other years and in other places they are older. The music at all-night vigils may be either a single guitarist or a music-and-dance group. Because musical groups and bands are often hired from different places, according to availability, reputation, and the tastes of the sponsors, different musical styles are possible. This is the case for the musicians at vigils, for the bands that play in processions, and for the music that accompanies the French and Apache dance dramas. Hymns and ballads sung at vigils are sometimes changed and new ones are created. The organizers, choreographers, and participants in crazies, giant puppet, plumed dance, and French and Apache performances are particularly inventive, surprising, and humorous and constantly seek to innovate. Each part of the fiesta has a certain flexibility, and the total structure of the fiesta is flexible. One year a bishop celebrates the mass, another year the priest does. One year a brass band plays "Las Mañanitas" in front of the parish church, another year it does not. Sometimes the visitors from San Luis de La Paz stay in Cruz del Palmar during the entire fiesta, sometimes they leave early. The number of vigils and their length are also flexible, though certain ones are obligatory.

The patron saint fiestas deploy social, cultural, and expressive elements, which, whatever their origins, are in a constant and dynamic states of development and change.

While we have focused on what happened in the New World after the conquest and up to the present, we should point out that these patron saint fiestas, which originated in Spain, are still going on there. They are part of Spanish culture. Many of the customs we documented in Mexico were described in a famous travelogue by British author Gerald Brenan about Andalusian villages between 1920 and 1934. The author marveled at processions, Moor and Christian dances, public singing and dancing, flower decorations, and collective meals. He even noted that musicians played slightly out of tune, as we have observed in Mexico.[58] The celebration of patron saints continues to this day in Spain. In May 2008, we observed fiestas in Cordova, Granada, and Madrid and were struck by the similarities to what we had observed in Mexico. These similarities included elaborate street processions with lavish displays of flowers, music, dances in honor of saints and crosses, fireworks and mock battles, giant puppets, and the intense participation of religious officials and many worshipers and bystanders. Since these customs, especially the dances, celebrate the Spanish conquest over and conversion of the Moors, they have to be adapted to the realities of contemporary Spain, which has an increasingly large North African population.

## IDENTITY

The practitioners of popular religion in Central Mexico, and especially in the fiestas of Cruz del Palmar and San Luis de la Paz, are typical representatives of deep Mexico. In skin color and other physical features, they can be considered indigenous. Psychologically, in their attitudes, beliefs, and self-position with respect to the rest of the world, they often consider themselves to be Indians. Socially and culturally, they are located along a continuum from Indian (representative of the pre-Columbian world) to Indo-Hispanic (representative of contemporary Mexico). Social and cultural features, along with physical features and mental self-representations, can be used to place people and their imagined, invented, and constructed identities along this continuum.[59] These social and cultural features include language, discourse styles and patterns, worldview and philosophy, dress, social organization, food products and their means of cultivation and culinary practices, economic practices, aesthetic traditions, and religious beliefs and practices, in particular patron saint fiestas.

While patron saint fiestas are about the expression of identity, especially the indigenous identity of deep Mexico, identity is not a static matter. Rather, it is the creative manipulation of a large number of expressive elements, nowhere more evident than with regard to religion and during patron saint fiestas. The French and Apache dances and dance dramas and the plumed dances are a striking example of a current, conscious, and active invention and reinvention of one aspect of their identity, their Indianness. People are interested in their own past and want to find out as much as possible about it. So choreographers for the local dance groups that perform at fiestas study books, magazines, television, and the Internet, converse with anthropologists and tourists, and use music, movement, dance, and clothing to construct Aztec, Chichimec, Otomi, or Apache identities, or creative combinations of these. The wild attire of some of the Chichimecs and Apaches might have been inspired by Powell's statement that the Chichimecs went to war barefleshed and with long hair painted red.[60]

Other moments during the fiesta enable people to display their Indianness. Individuals who speak Otomi in addition to Spanish but rarely use it have a greater tendency to use it during the fiesta. Men of Otomi origin who are involved in ritual activities sometimes wear white pants and shirts, along with sandals, even though these items of clothing are not particularly Otomi. Similarly, Chichimec women wear indigenous clothing in processions to express their Indianness, even though this clothing is not Chichimec clothing, which is no longer used, but rather that of other Mexican indigenous groups such as those of Tehuantepec or Yucatan. Fiestas, then, are occasions to be Indian, especially to construct and imagine oneself to be Indian, by drawing on a complex of expressive devices.[61] The double identity of Indo-Hispanics is constantly played out, enacted, and performed during the patron saint fiestas.

### FINAL WORDS

Patron saint fiestas are not about to disappear. They fill a crucial need for people in their lives and are becoming more and more exuberant, louder and louder. Fiestas will continue because of the system of fiesta leaders and officials (mayordomos and cargueros); because of their religious significance, the cult of the saints; because of their celebration of popular culture and history; because they are a way for people to express their identity; and because children are socialized into the culture of the fiesta and the adoration of the saints, and this stays with them all their lives. People feel deeply that patron saint fiestas are a precious inheritance and that honoring the patron saints is an obligation bequeathed to them by the ancestors. One might expect that consumerism will discourage the patron saint fiesta's ritual expenditures, and as a result these fiestas will disappear or be transformed into mere expressions of what some chamber of commerce wants.[62] But our experience is that this has not happened. Dedication to the patron saint is a way of life, an expression of identity, resistance, and religious fervor. It brings about a positive and effective sociability.[63] The patron saint fiesta is here to stay. Its practices, its imagery, its vocabulary, and its metaphors — performing the Four Winds (Cuatro Vientos) ceremony, perfuming with resin (copal), offering flowers and song (flor y canto) to the patron saints — permeate life, both private and public. Fiestas embody community, Indo-Hispanic identity, history, religion, and aesthetics.

# APPENDICES: CONTENTS

# A. APPENDICES TO CHAPTER ONE

## I. HISTORICAL BACKGROUND OF THE OTOMI

### Yolanda Lastra

*This section is a summary of Lastra (2006), which is a history of the Otomi that includes information on the history of the language, dialect differences, and the number of speakers from colonial times to the present.*

The place of origin of the Otomi is not known. Carrasco Pizana (1950) has proposed that Otomians originated in the Toluca Valley and the mountains to the north. From there they spread out and subdivided into the four groups that exist today: Otomi, Mazahua, Matlatzinca, and Ocuiltec. Soustelle, on the other hand, thinks they came from the Gulf coast. This is plausible because the oriental dialects of Otomi reflect the oldest stage of the language.

The ancestors of the Otomi were agriculturalists who lived in the central valleys of present-day Mexico. During the apogee of Teotihuacan (Early Classical period, AD 200–600) the Otomian languages started to diversify. Otomi as such has existed since the seventh century. Otomians in all probability were present in Teotihuacan, but archaeologists do not agree on what ethnic groups built and inhabited this cosmopolitan city.

After the fall of Teotihuacan, the northern part of the basin of Mexico and the plains to the north of Toluca were inhabited by Otomi and Mazahua. They also occupied Mezquital Valley, their most important center being Cahuacan to the south of Tepexi.

Around that time a type of ceramic called Coyotlatelco made its appearance; it is found in the basin of Mexico, Tula, and Tulancingo, but mainly in Azcapotzalco and Tenayuca. Its distribution fits the geographic area occupied by the Otomi. Tula was built in the center of a region that was mostly occupied by this people (Rattray 1996).

Tula was the most important state after the fall of Teotihuacan and before the rise of the Aztec city of Tenochtitlan. It was, apparently, multiethnic. Several authors, among them Jiménez Moreno (1954–1955), Motolinía (1941), and Davies (1977), point to the presence of Otomi in this city. After its fall (in 1175, according to Davies) they remained in the region.

The proposal of archaeologists such as Diehl (1983) and Mastache and Cobean (1989), who also suggested that the Otomi lived in Tula, has recently been confirmed by the findings of Fournier (1998) in Chapantongo, a political unit in the Tula region. Fournier and Vargas (2002) compared the DNA of Chapantongo burials with that of present-day Otomi and demonstrated that the individuals buried in the site were Otomi.

Jilotepec was an important Otomi area inhabited by them since 50 BC, according to Guerrero Guerrero (1983). Gerhard (1986) considers it to be an ancient kingdom that covered what is now the northwestern portion of the state of Mexico, the southwestern part of Hidalgo, and part of Querétaro. It is a vast territory where oriental and occidental Otomi meet. The Spanish friar Torquemada considered it the heart of their territory. It preserved its independence during the era of the Otomi kingdom of Xaltocan.

After the fall of Tula the Chichimec king Xolotl granted land to many peoples, among them Otomi from Jilotepec and Tepanecs comprising Matlatzinca, Otomi, and Mazahua from the Toluca Valley. One of the leaders of these peoples was Chiconcuah, who was given Xaltocan. The kingdom of Xaltocan flourished from 1220 to 1398. It included the Otomi region of the highlands of Puebla and Metztitlán, as well as the land inhabited by Mazahua, but not the Matlatzinca area (Nazareo 1940).

The wars in which Xaltocan took part are dealt with in Torquemada (1975). When the Mexica arrived in Chapultepec they were attacked by the people of Xaltocan. Ever since (1299), these peoples have been enemies. Later the people of Cuauthtitlán defeated those of Xaltocan in war, and their king fled to Metztitlán.

In the meantime, the Mexica had acquired more and more power. Their king, Izcoatl, and Nezahualcoyotl, king of Texcoco, assigned the Tepanec kingdom of Azcapotzalco formerly ruled by Maxtla to Tlacopan, thus founding the Triple Alliance, which was to govern a vast territory, including all of Central Mexico. Thereafter Tlacopan governed and obtained tribute from western and northern towns with Otomian peoples: all the western part of the basin of Mexico, the Toluca Valley (Matlatzinco and Mazahuacan), the province of Jilotepec, and the Teotlalpan, which is approximately what is now known as the Mezquital Valley.

Many of the former possessions of the Tepanecs had to be reconquered by the Triple Alliance. Almost the whole Otomi population became tributary to it except those who had taken refuge in Michoacán and Tlaxcala or who inhabited the independent states of Metztilán, Huayacocotla, and Tototepec. This was the approximate situation at the time of the arrival of the Spanish conquerors in 1519. Just as the hegemonic speakers of Nahuatl despised and ridiculed the Otomi, the European conquerors also looked down on them, and admired the Aztecs to a certain extent.

Cortés arrived in the independent kingdom of Tlaxcala, which had never been conquered by the Aztecs. He was attacked by Otomi warriors, who defended Tlaxcalan frontiers, but Spanish gunpowder prevailed over Otomi arrows. When the Tlaxcalan rulers were persuaded of the superiority of Spanish forces over their own, they decided to ally themselves with Cortés against Montezuma, the Aztec king, and consequently the whole of the Triple Alliance.

The cunning of Cortés, his intrepidity and treachery, are well-known, as is the result of the Spanish conquest. Less known is the important role played by the Otomi, who had been subject to the Triple Alliance and believed they could now free themselves by becoming allies of Cortés. Little did they know they would only be changing masters. But for a while, some of their leaders who were nobles fared well.

Under Spanish rule, the Otomi province of Jilotepec provided the conquerors with experienced warriors. The Otomi became conquerors themselves and founded towns such as Querétaro and San Juan del Río. Otomi expanded to the north. It was thus that many Otomi speakers later became peasants and miners in what are now the states of Querétaro and Guanajuato.

The Franciscan fray Juan de San Miguel, guardian of the convent of Acámbaro, arrived in the vicinity of what is now San Miguel de Allende at a site called Itzcuinapan (Nahuatl, meaning "on the water of the dogs") and built a modest church. He continued north, leaving fray Bernardo Cossin in charge. This friar built a better church with the help of the Otomi conqueror and founder of Querétaro, Hernando de Tapia. After the conversion of many Chichimec Indians, mostly Guamares, in San Miguel, Tlaxcalans were brought over, no doubt with Otomi among them. Later there were Purépechas as well.

According to local tradition, San Miguel was founded in 1531, but there is no record of an exact date of its founding (Wright 1993). The Spanish town was founded in 1555 on the order of viceroy Luis de Velasco. Indian governors were appointed, one for the Otomi and another for the Chichimecs and Tarascans (Purépechas) At first, San Miguel el Grande was part of Jilotepec province. It became a "villa" in 1559. After the founding of the villa of San Felipe in 1562, both towns formed a new *alcaldía*, "town with a mayor."

Many legends speak of the miracles that occurred and by means of which Chichimecs were conquered and baptized. There are also many documents narrating the exploits of Otomi conquerors and the founding of towns in both Querétaro and Guanajuato. It is hard to tell from these narratives what is historical and what is invention exalting the bravery of a given conqueror. Otomi continued to migrate from Central Mexico to this northern region; they were particularly attracted by the mines in Guanajuato during the first decades of the seventeenth century.

No doubt the expansion of the Spaniards to the north, attracted by the discovery of silver and other minerals, took place with Indian help, mainly that of Otomi warriors from Jilotepec. They had been subjected by the Mexica and wanted to make their own conquests, even if they had to play second fiddle to the Europeans. At first, Otomi leaders who had formed part of Indian nobility enjoyed many privileges because they had conquered Chichimecs and founded new towns for the Spanish Crown. As time went on, however, their descendants lost their privileges, and the conquests of their forefathers were forgotten.

The king of Spain and his royal officials were very much interested in the history of their newly acquired territories, in part because knowing the previous organization helped them exact tribute from their new subjects. In any case, there are numerous colonial documents preserved in Mexican and Spanish archives where one can learn about prehispanic and colonial history. Historians continue finding documents and reinterpreting the roles of the different peoples who became part of Spain's territory. But it is clear that the importance of the Otomi in the history of Central Mexico has been downplayed, and only recently have anthropologists and archaeologists begun to realize their outstanding contributions.

With independence from Spain, every Indian became a citizen, and consequently languages and ethnic groups are rarely mentioned as such. For instance, it is said that Indians supported Hidalgo in his struggle for independence, but we have to surmise which ones. It is thus difficult to study the Otomi as an entity.

Most Otomi groups are nominally Catholic, but many preserve old customs and beliefs, some of which may be prehispanic, while others were brought over by Spanish friars, soldiers, and other settlers. It is difficult to unravel what constitutes colonial and what constitutes pre-Columbian heritage in the popular religion (so called to distinguish it from orthodox Catholicism).

We know that after independence, most Otomi continued being farmers, but their land was constantly being taken away. Some preserved their language, but the number of speakers diminished as time went by. Spanish became the dominant language, the only one with prestige. As schools were founded, Spanish spread, and Indian languages were considered inferior by teachers, government officials, and monolingual speakers of Spanish in general. Very recently, cultural plurality and bilingualism have begun to be considered valuable officially. It remains to be seen whether present-day government policies will bear any fruit. It is perhaps only if the Indian communities themselves recognize the value of plurality that their identities will be preserved.

## REFERENCES

Benavente, fray Toribio de (Motolinía). 1941. *Historia de los indios de Nueva España*. Mexico City: Editorial Salvador Chávez Hayhoe.

Carrasco Pizana, Pedro. 1950. *Los Otomies: Cultura e historia prehispánica de los pueblos mesoamericanos de habla otomiana*. Facsimile edition. Mexico City: Biblioteca Enciclopédica del Estado de México, 1979.

Davies, Nigel. 1977. *The Toltecs, until the fall of Tula*. Norman: University of Oklahoma Press.

Diehl, Richard A. 1983. *Tula: The Toltec capital of ancient Mexico*. London: Thames and Hudson.

Fournier, Patricia. 1998. La luna del pie podrido: Simbolismo otomiano del siglo VII en la región de Tula. Paper presented at the Segundo Coloquio Estatal sobre Otopames, Pachuca, Hidalgo.

Fournier, Patricia, and Rocío Vargas Sanders. 2002. En busca de los "dueños del silencio": Cosmovisión y ADN antiguo de las poblaciones Otomies epiclásicas de la región de Tula. *Estudios de Cultura Otopame*, no. 3, 37–75. Mexico City: Instituto de Investigaciones Antropológicas, Universidad Nacional Autónoma de México.

Gerhard, Peter. 1986. *Geografía histórica de la Nueva España 1519–1821*. Mexico City: Universidad Nacional Autónoma de México.

Guerrero Guerrero, Raúl. 1983. *Los Otomies del valle del Mezquital.* Pachuca: Instituto Nacional de Antropología e Historia / Centro Regional Hidalgo.

Jiménez Moreno, Wigberto. 1954–1955. Síntesis de la historia precolonial del Valle de México. *Revista Mexicana de Estudios Antropológicos* 14:219–236.

Lastra, Yolanda. 2006. *Los Otomies: Su lengua y su historia.* Mexico City: Instituto de Investigaciones Antropológicas, Universidad Nacional Autónoma de México.

Mastache, Guadalupe, and Robert H. Cobean. 1985. Tula. In *Mesoamérica y el Centro de México,* ed. J. Monjarás Ruiz, R. Brambila, and E. Pérez Rocha, 273–307. Mexico City: Instituto Nacional de Antropología e Historia.

Nazareo, Pablo. 1940. Carta al rey don Felipe II, de don Pablo Nazareo de Xaltocan, 1566. Francisco del Paso y Troncoso, *Epistolario de Nueva España* 10:109–129.

Rattray, Evelyn. 1996. A regional perspective on the Epiclassic period in Central Mexico. In *Homenaje a William Sanders,* vol. 1, ed. G. Mastache, J. Parsons, R. Stanley, and M.C. Serra Puche, 213–231. Mexico City: Instituto Nacional de Antropología e Historia.

Torquemada, fray Juan de. 1975. *Monarquía Indiana.* Mexico City: Instituto de Investigaciones Históricas, Universidad Nacional Autónoma de México.

Wright, David. 1993. La conquista del Bajío y los orígenes de San Miguel de Allende. In *Memorias de la Academia Mexicana de la Historia,* vol. 36, *México,* 251–293. Mexico City: Academia Mexicana de la Historia.

## 2. HISTORICAL BACKGROUND OF THE CHICHIMECA JONAZ

### Yolanda Lastra

Early information on the Chichimeca Jonaz is scanty to nonexistent. They are referred to by the name Jonaces in the eighteenth century, although Gerhard (1986:63) in his section on Cadereyta speaks of a group of them living in its easternmost part, according to a document found in the Escorial library. Generally, however, before the eighteenth century they are referred to by the generic term Chichimec, which covers many other groups of hunters and gatherers (considered dangerous enemies by the Spaniards), as well as the ancestors of other peoples of Central Mexico.

Today the Chichimeca Jonaz live in the Misión de Chichimecas adjacent to the city of San Luis de la Paz in the state of Guanajuato. According to the 2000 census there are 1,641 speakers of their language, but their number is much lower than that, since children living in the area closer to the city do not speak it anymore.

Chichimeaco Jonaz is an Otopamean language. Its closest relative is Pame, which is spoken in a few communities in San Luis Potosí and Querétaro. The other Otopamean sub-branches are Otomi and Mazahua, on the one hand, and Matlatzinca and Ocuiltec on the other. Otopamean in turn is a branch of Otomanguean spoken mostly in Oaxaca.

At the time of the Spanish conquest, the center of Mexico was ruled by the Triple Alliance, formed by Mexico-Tenochtitlan, Tlacopan, and Tetzcoco. The lingua franca and the language used in government was Nahuatl. Tetzcoco was an important cultural center where Nahuatl was particularly cultivated, even though the population descended in part from Chichimecs brought by Xolotl, whom Carrasco (1950) considered to be Pames. The poet king Nezahualcoyotl had called himself *chichimeca tecuhtli,* "lord of the Chichimecs." To the north of the vast territory dominated by Nahuas there lived seminomadic hunters and gatherers whom the Spaniards called Chichimecs.

The Chichimec war began in 1547. When silver was discovered in Zacatecas, the conquerors needed to build roads through the territory of Indians who had never been subjected to a central power. Very little is known about their culture. Powell (1977) is the best reference on the war. What he says about the Chichimec way of life is mostly based on what he believed was written by Gonzalo las Casas, but it turns out that this captain was only in possession of a manuscript actually written by the Augustinian friar Guillermo de Santamaría, who had been a missionary to Guachichiles for many years (Santa María 2000)

The main groups of Chichimecs were Zacatecos, Guachichiles, Cazcanes, Guamares, and Pames. The latter were the least fierce, Guachichiles and Guamares the most warlike. The Copuces and their Guajaban and Sauza allies formed part of a Guamar confederation. It is interesting that most of these peoples except the Pames spoke Uto-Aztecan languages, but extremely little is known about them. The affiliation of Guamar to which Copuz and Guajaban seem to be related is not known.

The area of San Luis de la Paz was explored by the Franciscan friar Juan de San Miguel and by Juan Sanchez de Alanís, magistrate in Jilotepec. Guamar is spoken to the west and Pame to the east. In 1580 the Franciscans adopted the Doctrine of Sichú, and in 1590 Jesuits became in charge of San Luis de la Paz, bringing Otomis, Nahuas, and Tarascans with them. Although the town had been founded in 1552 (Ramírez 1952), we know nothing of its early history until the arrival of the Jesuits. They baptized Macolías, Guajabanes, and many Otomis and Spaniards. The predominant language was Guajabán. Consequently a catechism was written in it, but no trace of it remains.

According to Ramírez (1952), the viceroy Luis de Velasco granted the natives of San Luis de la Paz three sites for raising cattle. Who the "natives" were is not stated, but presumably they were Jonaces who had owned the sites previously, their former king Chupitantegua having granted land to them. This testimony has not been confirmed, and we do not know for sure whether or not there were Jonaces in San Luis de la Paz during viceroy Velasco's time, although according to oral history there were. The first baptismal records of Chichimecs are dated 1594.

On the other hand, it is certain that Jonaces lived in the Sierra Gorda and that in the first half of the eighteenth century they had not been subject to Spanish control. Friar Guadalupe Soriano discusses them in his *Prólogo Historial.* There were missions in Tolimán and San Juan Tecla, but the Jonaces escaped to the mountains. Then there was a mission in Maconí run by Dominicans, but the Chichimecs also fled. Later there was another mission in la Nopalera, also run by Dominicans; it lasted much longer but came to an end because of the savagery of the Spanish soldiers, who accused the Chichimecs of robbery, killed most, captured others, and sent them off to work in textile mills or in private homes, in the case of the women. The same was done in San José Vizarrón by order of José de Escandón. The remaining Jonaces fled to the mountains.

In Jiliapan, where Soriano lived, there were mostly Pames, but also some Jonaces. The archaeologist Viramontes Anzures (2000) notes that Jonaces reached as far as Zimapan, the puerto de la Media Luna, Tolimán, and Nopalera. Their favorite site was Cerro Prieto; another was the caves in Infiernillo, where the San Juan and Tula rivers join together. No Chichimecs remain in any of these places. They are remembered by the Otomi of San Miguel Tolimán, who attribute the origin of one of their dances to a Chichimec girl who worshipped the goddess of water in the form of a turtle (Piña Perusquía 1996).

In 1944 Vargas Rea published some documents from the archives in Queretaro about the Chichimecs. Here we learn more about the Spanish settlers' fear of and hatred for the Chichimecs and about the virtual extermination of the Chichimecs at the hands of Gabriel Guerrero de Ardila and José de Escandón.

From the extant documents it is clear that Chichimecs were present in many places besides the province of San Luis de la Paz, among them Zimapan; San José Vizarrón, Jalpan, Jiliapan, and Escanela in Cadereyta; and Tolimán in Querétaro. In the city of San Luis de la Paz they lived in the vicinity of the Sanctuary of the Virgin of Guadalupe, but gradually they were pushed to the mountainous and arid territory, where they now reside.

Until fairly recently Chichimecs from San Luis de la Paz traveled to Soriano on foot to visit the shrine of Our Lady of Soriano. This suggests they were aware of the common origin of the Jonaces of the former province of Cadereyta and themselves.

Chichimecs worked in haciendas and mines as day laborers until they were given land as a result of the revolution. Now they have an ejido, but many people sell their land to greedy mestizos. Their territory was divided by a highway constructed in the 1970s, and now the people who live closer to the town speak little Chichimec. They live in what is called Misión de Abajo. On the other side of the highway is the Misión de Arriba, where the language is spoken by most adults and some children.

There are two main traditional fiestas, the fiesta of Our Lady of Guadalupe and the fiesta of the patron saint, Saint Louis, king of France, which is the one we describe in this book.

## REFERENCES

Carrasco Pizana, Pedro. 1950. *Los Otomies: Cultura e historia prehispánica de los pueblos mesoamericanos de habla otomiana.* Facsimile edition. Mexico City: Biblioteca Enciclopédica del Estado de México, 1979.

Gerhard, Peter. 1986. *Geografía histórica de la Nueva España 1519–1821.* Mexico City: Universidad Nacional Autónoma de México.

Piña Perusquía, Abel. 1996. *La práctica religiosa Otomi: Procesos culturales de adaptación y cambio en Tolimán, Querétaro.* Thesis, Universidad Autónoma de Querétaro.

Powell, Philip W. 1977. *La guerra chichimeca.* Mexico City: Fondo de Cultura Económica.

Ramírez, Pbro. Esteban. 1952. *Estudio histórico de San Luis de la Paz, Guanajuato.* Photocopy. Archive, municipality of San Luis de la Paz.

Santa María, Guillermo de. 2000. *Guerra de los chichimecas* (México 1575–Zirosto 1580), ed. Alberto Carrillo Cázares. Zamora/Guanajuato, Mexico: El Colegio de Michoacán/ Universidad de Guanajuato.

Soriano, fray Juan Guadalupe. 1767. Difícil tratado del arte y unión de los idiomas othomii y pamee. Doctrina christiana, para la fácil enseñanza he intelligencia de los misterios de Ntra Santa Fe en el idioma pame, para bien de las almas. Manuscript. Benson Library, University of Texas, Austin.

Vargas Rea, ed. 1944. Pacificación de los chichimecas de la Sierra Gorda y dictamen del auditor de guerra marqués de Altamira. In *Biblioteca Aportación Histórica,* vol. 2. Mexico City: INAH, Archivo Histórico de Querétaro.

Viramontes Anzures, Carlos. 2000. *De chichimecas, pames y jonaces: Los recolectores cazadores del semidesierto de Querétaro.* Serie Arqueología. Mexico City: Instituto Nacional de Antropología e Historia.

# B. APPENDICES TO CHAPTER THREE

## I: HYMNS AND BALLADS (*ALABANZAS*)

*Recorded, transcribed, and translated by Yolanda Lastra*

### CON LICENCIA DE DIOS PADRE

(1) *Con licencia de Dios Padre*
*con licencia de Dios Hijo*
*con licencia de Dios el Espíritu Santo*

(2) *Formemos el primer viento*
*formemos el primer viento*
*del ánima de San Juan*
*del ánima de San Juan*
*que en el Evangelio está.*

(3) *Formando el segundo viento*
*formando el segundo viento*
*del ánima de San Lucas*
*del ánima de San Lucas*
*que en el Evangelio está.*

(4) *Formemos el tercer viento*
*formemos el tercer viento*
*del ánima de San Mateo*
*del ánima de San Mateo*
*que en el Evangelio está.*

(5) *Formemos el cuarto viento*
*formemos el cuarto viento*

*del ánima de San Marcos*
*del ánima de San Marcos*
*que en el Evangelio está.*

*(6) En los cielos y en la tierra*
*en los cielos y en la tierra*
*está el poderoso Dios*
*y el Santísimo Sacramento*
*está en el altar.*

*(7) Él es Dios*
*y las ánimas benditas*
*del santo purgatorio.*

*(8) Que viva l'ánima sola*
*que viva l'ánima sola*
*que está en la Catedral*
*que está en la Catedral*
*de México.*

*(9) Que viva Señor Santiago*
*que viva Señor Santiago*
*porque él es el correo*
*porque él es el correo*
*de los Cuatro Vientos.*

*(10) Ánimas conquistadoras*
*sabe Dios dónde estarán*
*ánimas conquistadoras*
*sabe Dios dónde estarán*
*todos roguemos por ellas*
*todos roguemos por ellas*
*que en gloria descansen en paz*
*que en gloria descansen en paz.*

*(11) Alma de María Francisca*
*sabe Dios dónde estará*
*alma de María Francisca*
*sabe Dios dónde estará*
*todos roguemos por ella*
*todos roguemos por ella*
*que en gloria descansen en paz*
*que en gloria descansen en paz.*

(12) *Alma de los mayordomos*
*sabe Dios dónde estará*
*alma de los mayordomos*
*sabe Dios dónde estará*
*todos roguemos por ella*
*todos roguemos por ella*
*que en gloria descansen en paz*
*que en gloria descansen en paz.*

[Mayordomo:] *El es Dios.*
[Todos:] *El es dios.*

## With Permission from God the Father

(1) With permission from God the Father
with permission from God the Son
with permission from God the Holy Spirit.

(2) Let us form the first wind
let us form the first wind
to the soul of Saint John
to the soul of Saint John
who is in the Gospel.

(3) Forming the second wind
forming the second wind
to the soul of Saint Luke
to the soul of Saint Luke
who is in the Gospel.

(4) Let us form the third wind
let us form the third wind
to the soul of Saint Matthew
to the soul of Saint Matthew
who is in the Gospel.

(5) Let us form the fourth wind
let us form the fourth wind
to the soul of Saint Mark
to the soul of Saint Mark
who is in the Gospel.

(6) In heaven and on earth
in heaven and on earth

is the powerful God
and the Holy Sacrament
is on the altar.

(7) He is God
and the blessed souls
of purgatory.

(8) Long live the lonely soul
long live the lonely soul
who is in the Cathedral
who is in the Cathedral
of Mexico.

(9) Long live Lord St. James
long live Lord St. James
because he is the messenger
because he is the messenger
of the Four Winds,

(10) Conqueror souls
only God knows where they may be
conqueror souls
only God knows where they may be
let us pray for them
let us pray for them
so in Glory they may rest in peace
so in Glory they may rest in peace.

(11) Soul of María Francisca
only God knows where she may be
soul of María Francisca
only God knows where she may be.

(12) Souls of the fiesta leaders
only God knows where they may be
souls of the fiesta leaders
only God knows where they may be
let us pray for them
let us pray for them
so in Glory they may rest in peace
so in Glory they may rest in peace.

[Fiesta leader:] He is God.
[Everyone:] He is God.

## La gran Tenochtitlán

(1) *Cuando nuestra América*
*fue conquistada*
*de todos los habitantes*
*ninguno vido nada*
*allá en la gran en la gran Tenochtitlán.*

(2) *Cuando Hernán Cortés*
*entró por el Peñón*
*fundó la conquista*
*de la religión*
*allá en la gran en la gran Tenochtitlán.*

(3) *Cuando Hernán Cortés*
*salió por el Peñón*
*fue a darle el encuentro*
*a Cristobal Colón*
*allá en la gran en la gran Tenochtitlán*

(4) *Cuando Cuauhtemoc*
*como fiel guerrero*
*llega a la acción*
*y lo hace[n] prisionero*
*allá en la gran en la gran Tenochtitlán.*

(5) *Cuando nuestra América*
*fue conquistada*
*la reina Malinche*
*fue bautizada*
*allá en la gran en la gran Tenochtitlán.*

(6) *Cuando la Malinche*
*fue bautizada*
*de todos los habitantes*
*ninguno vido nada*
*allá en la gran en la gran Tenochtitlán.*

(7) *Cuando nuestro reino*
*fue conquistado*

*los indios chichimecas*
*fueron bautizados*
*allá en la gran en la gran Tenochtitlán.*

(8) *En ese Santiago*
*Santiago de Querétaro*
*en el año mil quinientos*
*quinientos treinta y uno*
*allá en la gran en la gran Tenochtitlán.*

(9) *En ese cerrillo*
*cerrillo de San Grimál* [sic]
*donde corrió la sangre*
*hasta el arenal*
*allá en la gran en la gran Tenochtitlán.*

(10) *Cuando nuestra América*
*fue conquistada*
*de todos los habitants ninguno vido nada.*
*Cuando nuestra América*
*fue conquistada*
*de todos los habitants ninguno vido nada*
*allá en la gran en la gran Tenochtitlán*
*allá en la gran en la gran Tenochtitlán.*

## The Great Tenochtitlán

(1) When our America
was conquered
with all its inhabitants
no one saw anything
over there in the great Tenochtitlán.

(2) When Hernán Cortés
entered by the Peñón
he founded the conquest
of religion
over there in the great Tenochtitlán.

(3) When Hernán Cortés
departed by the Peñón
Christopher Colombus
went to meet him
over there in the great Tenochtitlán.

(4) When Cuauhtemoc
as a loyal warrior
came to battle
he was taken prisoner
over there in the great Tenochtitlán.

(5) When our America
was conquered
Queen Malinche
was baptized
over there in the great Tenochtitlán.

(6) When Malinche
was baptized
with all its inhabitants
no one saw anything
over there in great Tenochtitlán.

(7) When our kingdom
was conquered
the Chichimec Indians
were baptized
over there in the great Tenochtitlán.

(8) In this Santiago
Santiago of Querétaro
in the year fifteen hundred
fifteen hundred and thirty-one
over there in the great Tenochtitlán.

(9) On that hill
the hill of San Grimal
blood flowed
down to the sandy ground
over there in the great Tenochtitlán.

(10) When our America
was conquered
none of its inhabitants saw anything.
When our America
was conquered
none of its inhabitants saw anything
over there in the great Tenochtitlán
over there in the great Tenochtitlán.

## Señor de Villaseca

(1) *Año de mil ochocientos*
*noventa y uno contaba.*
*El señor de Villaseca*
*libró a una mujer casada.*

(2) *Se levantó su marido*
*a trabajar amellado*
*hoy que nos valga la muerte*
*las llagas de su costado*

(3) *La mujer a la confianza*
*que se había ido a trabajar*
*compuso la canastilla*
*y se fue a dar de almorzar.*

(4) *Agarró la canastilla*
*ay por la Cata bajó.*
*Para su mala desgracia*
*a su marido encontró.*

(5) *Le preguntó su marido*
*a dónde vas mujer ingrata*
*hoy te he dejado en tu casa*
*dime mujer qué te falta.*

(6) *Le responde la mujer*
*que los labios se la secan,*
*voy a llevarle estas flores*
*al Señor de Villaseca.*

(7) *Con la punta del puñal*
*levantó la servilleta*
*estaba la canastilla*
*toda de flores cubierta.*

(8) *Las tortillas eran flores*
*el salero era el somerio*
*los granitos de la sal*
*las penas del cautiverio.*

(9) *Por esa calle derecha*
*que le nombran la Plazuela*

*la cuchara que llevaba*
*era una vela de sebo.*

(10) *Anda y llévale las flores.*
*a ese divino señor*
*y dile que nos perdone*
*las faltas del corazón.*

(11) *En las puertas del convento*
*la mujer se arrodilló.*
*El Señor de Villaseca*
*de flores la coronó.*

(12) *De las puertas para adentro*
*la mujer se arrodilló.*
*El Señor de Villaseca*
*de flores la coronó.*

(13) *De las puertas para adentro*
*el hombre se arrodilló.*
*El Señor de Villaseca*
*el intento le quitó.*

(14) *Y el diablo que no duerme*
*vive de sus aventuras*
*en una mujer casada*
*goza de sus travesuras.*

(15) *En medio del cementerio*
*está una florida seca*
*quedaron las maravillas*
*del Señor de Villaseca.*

(16) *En el mineral de Cata*
*a donde habita el Señor*
*ay detrás del camerín*
*el retablo se quedó.*

(17) *En fin yo ya me despido*
*del reloj y su campanada.*
*El Señor de Villaseca*
*libró a una mujer casada.*

(18) *Ya con esta me despido*
*a la orilla de una loma.*
*Vamos a darle las gracias*
*a esta divina paloma.*

(19) *Ya con esta me despido*
*del reloj y su campanada.*
*El Señor de Villaseca*
*libró a una mujer casada.*

(20) *Ya con ésta me despido*
*a la orilla de una acequia.*
*Quedaron las maravillas*
*del Señor de Villaseca.*

(21) *En medio del cementerio*
*stá una florida seca.*
*Estas son las maravillas*
*del Señor de Villaseca.*

(22) *Año de mil ochocientos*
*noventa y un contaba.*
*El Señor de Villaseca*
*libró a una mujer casada.*

## Lord of Villaseca

(1) Year eighteen hundred
ninety-one had been counted.
The Lord of Villaseca
saved a married woman.

(2) Her husband
got up troubled to go to work
so death would be worth
the wounds in His side.

(3) The woman trusting
he had gone to work
fixed her basket
and left to take lunch [to her lover].

(4) She took the basket
and went down toward Cata.

It was her misfortune
to meet up with her husband

(5) Her husband asked:
Where are you going ungrateful woman?
Haven't I left you at home?
Tell me what you need.

(6) His wife answers
with her lips drying up,
I'm taking these flowers
to the Lord of Villaseca.

(7) With the tip of his dagger
he raised the napkin
and saw the basket
full of flowers.

(8) The tortillas had become flowers
the salt-cellar a resin burner
and the grains of salt
the grief of captivity.

(9) Through that straight street
called Plazuela
the spoon she had taken
had become a tallow candle.

(10) Go take the flowers
to that divine Lord
and tell him to forgive
the sins in our hearts.

(11) At the gates of the convent
the woman knelt down.
The Lord of Villaseca
crowned her with flowers.

(12) Inside the gates
the woman knelt down.
The Lord of Villaseca
crowned her with flowers.

(13) Inside the gates
the man knelt down.
The Lord of Villaseca
removed his intent.

(14) And the devil who doesn't sleep
lives from his adventures
rejoices in the tricks
of a married woman.

(15) In the midst of the cemetery
there is a dry flower bed.
There remained the marvels
Of the Lord of Villaseca.

(16) There in the mine of Cata
where the Lord lives
behind the side chapel
her drawing giving thanks remained.

(17) With this song I'll take my leave
of the clock and its striking.
The Lord of Villaseca
saved a married woman.

(18) With this song I'll take my leave
on the edge of a small hill.
Let us thank
that holy dove.

(19) With this song I'll take my leave
of the clock and its striking.
The Lord of Villaseca
saved a married woman.

(20) With this song I'll take my leave
by the side of a ditch.
These are the marvels
of the Lord of Villaseca.

(21) In the midst of the cemetery
there is a dry flower bed.
There remained the marvels
of the Lord of Villaseca.

(22) Year eighteen hundred
ninety-one had been counted.
The Lord of Villaseca
saved a married woman.

## Van los concheros de dos en dos

(1) *Van los concheros de dos en dos*
*como diciendo el nombre de Dios.*
*El copalito y el somador*
*bien preparados deben estar.*

(2) *Van los concheros de dos en dos*
*como diciendo el nombre de Dios.*
*Las florecitas*
*bien preparadas deben estar.*
*El ramillete y la cucharilla*
*clarín de marcha retornará.*

## *The Musicians Go Two by Two*

(1) The musicians go two by two
as if they were invoking God's name.
The little resin and the resin burner
have to be well prepared.

(2) The musicians go two by two
as if they were invoking God's name.
The little flowers
have to be well prepared.
The altarpiece and the desert spoon
the bugle for a march will come back.

## Año de mil nuevecientos

(1) *Año de mil nuevecientos*
*nuevecientos treinta y cuatro*
*nos persiguieron los templos*
*en l'estado de Guanajuato.*

(2) *Decía el cura de Celaya*
*ya por el amor de Dios*
*ya van a tumbar un templo.*

(3) *El señor cura decía*
*cómo le vamos a hacer?*
*Cambiaremos la reliquia*
*al templo de la Merced.*

(4) *Decía el cura de Celaya*
*como duele el corazón.*

(5) *Al obispo de Morelia*
*le mandaron avisar.*
*en la ciudad de Celaya*
*un templo iban a tumbar.*

(6) *El obispo de Morelia*
*contestó a la capital*
*en la ciudad de Celaya*
*un templo iban a tumbar.*

(7) *Para poderlo tumbar*
*se valieron del gobierno*
*del gobierno federal.*

## The Year of Nineteen Hundred

(1) The year of nineteen hundred
nineteen hundred and thirty-four
they persecuted the temples
in the state of Guanajuato.

(2) The parish priest of Celaya said
for the love of God
they are going to take down a temple.

(3) The priest said
what are we going to do?
Let's move the relics
to the church of La Merced.

(4) The priest of Celaya was saying
how much our hearts hurt.

(5) The bishop of Morelia
was warned

that in the city of Celaya
a temple would be torn down.

(6) The bishop of Morelia
answered the capital
in the city of Celaya
a temple would be torn down.

(7) In order to tear it down
they made use of the government
of the federal government.

## Señor de Esquipula

(1) *Señor de Esquipula*
*mi padre querido*
*al venir al mundo*
*fuiste aparecido.*

(2) *Tan humilde fuiste*
*O Cristo sagrado*
*que le apareciste*
*a un hombre casado.*

(3) *El hombre dichoso*
*luego que lo vio*
*lo tomó en sus manos*
*y luego se lo llevó.*

(4) *La mujer ingrata*
*luego que lo vio*
*lo tomó en sus manos*
*y luego lo quemó.*

(5) *Esto fue a las diez*
*cuando lo quemó.*
*Para el medio día*
*loba se volvió.*

(6) *La dejó el Señor*
*para su venganza,*
*loba para siempre*
*y sin esperanza.*

(7) *De los aullidos*
*que esa loba daba*
*toditito el pueblo*
*se atemorizaba.*

(8) *Tan humilde fuiste*
*O Cristo sagrado.*
*En terribles llamas*
*y no te has quemado.*

(9) *Pareces la luna*
*pareces el sol*
*tú nos iluminas*
*con tu resplandor.*

(10) *Pareces el sol*
*pareces la luna*
*tú nos iluminas*
*señor de Esquipulas.*

(11) *Señor de Esquipulas*
*tu divina luz*
*donde te veneras*
*en la Santa Cruz.*

(12) *Bendita ciudad*
*queretana*
*que escogió el Señor*
*para su morada.*

## Lord of Esquipula

(1) Lord of Esquipula
my beloved father
when you came to the world
you came like a ghost

(2) You were so humble
O sacred Christ
that you appeared
to a married man.

(3) The happy man
as soon as he saw him

166

took him in his hands
and carried him away.

(4) The ungrateful woman
as soon as she saw him
took him in her hands
and burned him immediately.

(5) This was at ten
when she burned him.
By noon
she had turned into a wolf.

(6) The Lord let her be a wolf
in revenge,
a wolf forever
without hope.

(7) Because of the howling
of this wolf
the whole town
was in fear.

(8) You were so humble
O sacred Christ.
In terrible flames
you did not burn.

(9) You are like the moon
you are like the sun
you lighten us
with your shining light.

(10) You are like the moon
you are like the sun
you lighten us
Lord of Esquipula.

(11) Lord of Esquipula
your divine light
where you are worshiped
on the Holy Cross.

(12) Blessed city
Querétaro
that the Lord chose
for his abode.

## Estrella del Oriente

(1) *Estrella del Oriente*
*que nos das tu santa luz.*
*Ya es hora que sigamos*
*el camino de la Cruz.*

(2) *Oriente es el primer viento*
*que debemos conquistar*
*el ánima de San Juan*
*en el Evangelio está.*

(3) *Poniente es el segundo viento*
*que debemos conquistar*
*el ánima de San Lucas*
*en el Evangelio está.*

(4) *Sur es el tercer viento*
*que debemos conquistar*
*el ánima de San Mateo*
*en el Evangelio está.*

(5) *Norte es el cuarto viento*
*que debemos conquistar*
*el ánima de San Marcos*
*en el Evangelio está.*

(6) *Malinche abanderada*
*de todo corazón*
*ya tomó la disciplina*
*para darle ejecución.*

(7) *Salió Cuauhtemotzin*
*y Carlos V también*
*revoloteando el estandarte*
*de la Malinche Isabel.*

(8) *Somemos los cuatro vientos*
*con este somador.*

*Y besémonos las manos*
*y digamos, "Él es Dios".*

*(9) Ordene sus alferez,*
*nos dice el general.*
*Y amémonos compadres,*
*nos decía el caudillo real.*

*(10) Caminemos presurosos*
*a nombre de Jesús*
*y la estrella del Oriente*
*de la santa cruz.*

*(11) Adentro indios flecheros!*
*Les gritaba Hernán Cortés.*
*Pongan bien sus escudos*
*Al español y al francés!*

*(12) Brillen bien sus escudos*
*Y opaquen la maldad!*
*Que ay vienen ya los turcos*
*En contra de la Cristiandad!*

*(13) Las hondas y las flechas*
*ya todas en prevención.*
*Al viento van las jaras*
*peleando la religión.*

*(14) Malinche abanderada*
*de todo corazón.*
*Y las conchas de armadillo*
*proclamando bien su afán.*

*(15) En una noche triste*
*y un árbol a sus pies*
*se hallaba ay llorando*
*el ánima de Hernán Cortés.*

*(16) Pueblito de Tlaxcala*
*no se me puede olvidar*
*Porque ay quedó firmada*
*La palabra general.*

## Star of the East

(1) Star of the East
you give us your sacred light.
It is time for us to follow
the way of the Cross.

(2) East is the first wind
we must conquer
the soul of Saint John
who is in the Gospel.

(3) West is the second wind
we must conquer
the soul of Saint Luke
who is in the Gospel.

(4) South is the third wind
we must conquer
the soul of Saint Matthew
who is in the Gospel.

(5) North is the fourth wind
we must conquer
the soul of Saint Mark
who is in the Gospel.

(6) Malinche carrying the flag
with all her heart
has taken the whip
to flagellate herself.

(7) Cuauhtemoc came out
and so did Charles V
waving the banner
of Malinche (queen) Isabel.

(8) Let us perfume the Four Winds
with this resin burner.
Let us kiss each other's hands
and say, "He is God."

(9) Order your standard bearers,
the general tells us.

Let us love one another,
said the royal chief.

(10) Let us walk quickly
in the name of Jesus
and the star of the East
of the Holy Cross.

(11) Inside you Indians armed with bows and arrows!
shouted Hernán Cortés.
With your shields
protect the Spanish and the French!

(12) Brighten well your shields
and darken evil!
Here come the Turks
fighting Christianity!

(13) Slingshots and arrows
are all ready.
Arrows fly through the wind
fighting for religion.

(14) Malinche with her flag
and willing heart.
And the armadillo shells
proclaim their eagerness.

(15) A sad night
at the foot of a tree
was the crying soul
of Hernán Cortés.

(16) Little town of Tlaxcala
I cannot forget
because there was signed
the general word.

## 2: EXCERPTS FROM A RITUAL LEADER'S SPEECH AT THE END OF THE VIGIL OF THE DESERT SPOON (*VELACIÓN DE LA CUCHARILLA*), CRUZ DEL PALMAR, DECEMBER 30–31, 1997

*El es Dios.*

*Bueno, queridos compadritos, ya terminamos el trabajo de hacer ese ramillete, ustedes lo ven. Por todos nosotros, por todos los cargueros, esperando que Dios nuestro señor y la Santísima Virgen y demás imágenes que la acompañan alrededor, damos las gracias y hasta el venidero, si Dios nos da licencia, estaremos en este lugar, los que vívamos, sea por Dios, porque la vida, de un rato a otro nos llegará nuestro fin a cada quien. Por la intención de todos nosotros, vamos a rezarle un Padre Nuestro y un Ave María a este santo trabajo, este santo lugar.*

*Padre Nuestro*

*Ave María*

*Gloria*

*Por la intención de aquellas almas que ya se fueron ya, más adelante principalmente por aquella alma de* [mentions former *mayordomos* and *tenanchas* by name] *María Hilaria, José Ricardo, José Crispín, José Antonio y todos los demás.*

He is God.

Well, dear ritual kin, now we have finished the work of making this altarpiece, as you see. For all of us, for all the fiesta officials, hoping God our Lord, the most holy Virgin, and all the other images that accompany [us] all around, we give thanks. Until next year when, God willing, we will be here, those of us who may be alive. For the sake of God, because life, from one moment to the next, the end will come to each of us.

For our intentions, let us pray an Our Father and a Hail Mary for the sake of this holy work, this holy place.

Our Father

Hail Mary

Gloria

For the intentions of the departed souls who preceded us, especially for the souls of [mentions former mayordomos and tenanchas by name; each woman's name is preceded by "María" and each man's name by "José"] María Hilaria, José Ricardo, José Crispín, José Antonio, and all the others.

Our Father

Hail Mary

Gloria

## 3: HYMN TO THE SAINTS AT THE VIGIL OF THE FIESTA OFFICIALS (*VELACIÓN DE LOS CARGUEROS*), CRUZ DEL PALMAR, JANUARY 5–6, 1998

(1) *Ay Santo Entierrito como tú lo ves,*
*aquí nos ponemos postrados a tus pies.*
*Ay Santo Entierrito como tú lo ves,*
*aquí nos ponemos postrados a tus pies.*
*Por eso te pido Padre de mi amor,*
*que no eches al olvido a este pecador.*

(2) *Jesús Nazareno como tú lo ves,*
*aquí nos ponemos postrados a tus pies.*
*Jesús Nazareno como tú lo ves,*
*aquí nos ponemos postrados a tus pies.*
*Por eso te pido, Padre de mi amor*
*que no eches al olvido a este pecador.*

(3) *Santísima Virgen como tú lo ves,*
*aquí nos ponemos postrados a tus pies.*
*Santísima Virgen como tú lo ves,*
*aquí nos ponemos postrados a tus pies.*
*Por eso te pido Madre de mi amor,*
*que no eches al olvido a este pecador.*

(4) *Santísima cruz como tú lo ves,*
*aquí nos ponemos postrados a tus pies.*
*Santísima cruz como tú lo ves,*
*aquí nos ponemos postrados a tus pies.*
*Por eso te pido, Madre de mi amor,*
*que no eches al olvido a este pecador.*

(1) O Holy Burial as you see it,
here we have prostrated ourselves at your feet.
O Holy Burial as you see it,
here we have prostrated ourselves at your feet.
For this reason I ask you, Father of my love,
not to throw this sinner into oblivion.

(2) Jesus of Nazareth as you see it,
here we have prostrated ourselves at your feet.
Jesus of Nazareth as you see it,
here we have prostrated ourselves at your feet.

For this reason I ask you, Father of my love,
not to throw this sinner into oblivion.

(3) Holy Virgin as you see it,
here we have prostrated ourselves at your feet.
Holy Virgin as you see it,
here we have prostrated ourselves at your feet.
For this reason I ask you, Mother of my love,
not to throw this sinner into oblivion.

(4) Holy Cross as you see it,
here we have prostrated ourselves at your feet.
Holy Cross as you see it,
here we have prostrated ourselves at your feet.
For this reason I ask you, Mother of my love,
not to throw this sinner into oblivion.

## 4. EXCERPTS OF SPEECHES BY A FIESTA LEADER AND ONE OF THE FIESTA OFFICIALS AT THE VIGIL OF THE FIESTA OFFICIALS (*VELACIÓN DE LOS CARGUEROS*), CRUZ DEL PALMAR, JANUARY 6–7, 1998

Fiesta leader

*Pues hemos cumplido con nuestras tradiciones la devoción de esta Santa Mesa. Le damos gracias a los cargueros que nos hicieron el favor de acompañarnos rogando a Nuestro Padre, Señor Santo Entierro, Nuestro Padre Jesús Nazareno, y a la Santísima Virgen de los Dolores. Quizá y Dios quiera hoy mismo en la noche [6-1 para amanecer el 7-1], sea posible de que salgan estos cargos (ahí estaban las roscas de los que faltaban), que haiga voluntarios por ay para que así reciban los nuevos pal venidero. Los que vívamos aquí estaremos en este lugar, y los que no puse que sea lo que Dios diga. Porque la vida la tenemos prestada, la muerte llega de un rato a otro, sea chico, sea grande, de todos modos es camino que todos llevamos. Por nuestra parte, muchísimas gracias compadritos, concheros que acompañan aquí a los cargueros principalmente, y el carguero quien es carguero y conchero a la vez.*

Fiesta official:

*A nombre de todas las ánimas, las del purgatorio principalmente, todas aquellas almas, aquellas tenanchas, que con tantas lágrimas nos dejaron estas santas tradiciones, aque- llos sargentos, que vinieron a poner la primera piedra, en donde prendieron su lumbre para prender su somador, en donde aquellos entonces derramaron sus lágrimas, aquellos sargentos, por plantar esta santa piedra donde estamos hoy, en esta parroquia que hoy es parroquia.*

Fiesta leader

Well, we have accomplished with our traditions the devotion of this Holy Board. We give thanks to the fiesta officials who were kind enough to come with us and pray to Our Father, the Lord Holy Burial, Our Lord Father Jesus of Nazareth, and Our Lady of Sorrows. Perhaps God willing tonight [Jan 6–7], people will accept the duties (here were the breads of those who were missing [see chapter four]). Perhaps there will be volunteers somewhere, so that they will take charge next year. Those of us who live will be here, and those who won't, well, let it be the will of God. Because life is a loan, death will be here in a while, a short one or a long one, but our path is the same. For our part, thank you compadritos, players of the armadillo shell who are here to accompany the fiesta officials, and the fiesta official who is both fiesta official and armadillo shell player.

The fiesta official just mentioned says:

In the name of the departed souls, those in purgatory mainly, all of those souls, the female ritual leaders, who with abundant tears left us these traditions, the sargents who came to lay the first stone, where they kindled their fires to light their resin burner, where they then shed tears, such sargents who lay the holy stone where we stand now in this church, now a parish church.

### 5. EXCERPTS FROM A SPEECH BY A RITUAL LEADER AT A VIGIL, SAN LUIS DE LA PAZ, SEPTEMBER 3, 1999

The ritual leader is addressing the people gathered for the vigil. He quotes from and comments on a text that he had acquired at another ritual gathering. There is an alternation among the speaker quoting the text (we placed this in quotation marks), the speaker providing his own commentary on the text, and the speaker describing what is taking place at the current vigil. Sections of the speech praise God with the phrase "He is God" (*El es Dios*), which is uttered by the speaker and responded to by the participants in the vigil.

*Con todo respeto, una Comisión del pueblo de Xichú allá en Victoria, Guanajuato se une al júbilo que embarga a la tradición de los san miguelenses, en el aniversario de la fundación de este pueblo por fray Juan de San Miguel. Físicamente él ya no existe con nosotros, pero su espíritu preside en este acto. En la tradición de Sierra Gorda el altar de ofrendas a nuestros seres queridos, que se nos adelantaron en el viaje que no tiene retorno, está siempre en tres planos, que simbolizan las tres dimensiones en el plano terrestre, todos precedidos por la cruz de dos líneas que se interceptan en un punto central, siendo símbolos del equilibrio de las fuerzas cósmicas. Además, cinco cruces que indican nuestros pasos por este mundo, cinco cruces sobre el cuadrilátero sagrado, un petate que representa el plano terrestre son los que nos muestran el recorrido del ser hacia la luz divina. La primera cruz de sal nos dice que al venir a este mundo, llegamos preservados o preparados para no corrompernos, pues por este medio de la salación nuestro cuerpo físico durará mucho tiempo en buen estado. Podemos así cumplir nuestra misión en la tierra.*

*El es Dios.*

*El es Dios.*

*Horita pasará la niña a dar a que tomen la sal. La necesitamos para nuestras comidas, para todo. Entonces contemplemos en esta ceremonias que ésta es una cosa sagrada. Debemos tomar un granito de sal y hacernos la cruz, para invocarle al señor lo que estamos haciendo en esta ceremonia.*

*El es Dios.*

*El es Dios.*

*Entonces dice: "La cruz de tierra simboliza el seno de nuestra madre, Ella nos depara el sustento. A ella la necesitamos en nuestra existencia. Y a ella torna nuestro cuerpo físico al venir la muerte."*

*El es Dios.*

*El es Dios.*

*Podemos pensar que también los sacerdotes nos dicen en la ceniza que ceniza somos y a ceniza tenemos que llegar.*

*Entonces eso es lo de la tierra, que es nuestra madre. Ella nos da de comer, nos sustenta, nos da el sustento. Todo esto es una cosa sagrada en nuestras tradiciones.*

*De ceniza es la tercera cruz, símbolo de que cenizas somos, de que como tributo nuestra materia debe reintegrarse a su origen, a la tierra.*

*Así en base a nuestros trabajos y a nuestras buenas obras, haremos merecedores de las flores de la cuarta cruz. La cruz de las flores es la que nos conduce, de acuerdo a nuestros merecimientos, a la quinta cruz.*

*El es Dios.*

*El es Dios.*

*Esa es la cruz de las flores.*

*La cruz de la luz, símbolo de divinidad, del centro, el arriba y el abajo, el fuego interno que es el que nos da el poder, que nos hace hombres, y que nos permite por medio del copal consumir nuestras lágrimas y ofrecerlas en aromas agradables al dador de la vida.*

*Fíjense no más lo que dice, "que con l'aroma del copal, con el aigre, es un intermediador para nosotros en estas ceremonias. Tienen que llegar nuestras pláticas que estamos haciendo, por ejemplo, horita a Nuestro Señor pidiéndole de corazón en nuestras tradiciones."*

*Los manjares y las frutas se nos representan el alimento necesario para alimentar la envoltura o cuerpo físico del espíritu. Eso es para nosotros, para la humanidad. Este tipo de velaciones es siempre acompañado de un grupo coral. Sus labores en el Altísimo son para implorar benevolencia para el espíritu que deja la materia.*

*Entonces, ese tipo de velaciones, con el grupo coral, viene ser por eso ahorita, nosotros que estamos con nuestras conchas haciendo la ceremonia, cantándole alabanzas al señor, venerándolo y alabándolo en sus tradiciones. Eso es lo que significan estas cosas, para que no vayan a interpretar mal, que vamos a hacer otras cosas.*

*El es Dios, compadritos.*

*El es Dios.*

With all respect, a commission from the town of Xichú up in Victoria, Guanajuato, joins in the rejoicing of the people of San Miguel, bound in the tradition of celebrating the anniversary of the foundation of this town by Friar Juan de San Miguel. He no longer exists physically with us, but his spirit presides over this act. In the tradition of the Sierra Gorda, the altar with offerings to our loved ones, who preceded us on the trip that has no return, is always on three planes, which symbolize three dimensions on the terrestrial plane, all preceded by the cross with two lines that intercept each other at a central point, symbolizing the equilibrium of cosmic forces. Furthermore, five crosses that indicate our steps in this world, five crosses on the sacred quadrilateral, a straw mat that represents the terrestrial plane, are those that show us the path of being toward the holy light. The first cross of salt tells us that in coming into this world, we arrived preserved or prepared to not be corrupted, because by means of salation our physical body will last a long time in good condition. We can thus fulfill our mission in life.

He is God.

He is God.

Now a girl will come by so that you can take salt. We need it for our food, for everything. So let us look on these ceremonies as something sacred. We must take a grain of salt and cross ourselves to invoke God and tell him what we are doing during this ceremony.

He is God.

He is God.

Then it [the text] says, "The cross of earth symbolizes the bosom of our mother. She gives us food. We need her throughout our existence. And our bodies go back to her when death comes."

He is God.

He is God.

We can think that also the priests tell us that we are ashes and to ashes we must return.

So this is from the Earth, who is our mother. She feeds us, she sustains us, she gives us sustenance. All of this is sacred in our traditions.

"Of ashes is the third cross, symbol of the ashes that we are, of the contribution of our flesh, which must return to its origin, earth.

"Thus on the basis of our works and our good deeds, we will become worthy of the flowers of the fourth cross. The cross of flowers is the one that leads us, according to our merits, to the fifth cross."

He is God.

He is God.

That is the cross of the flowers.

"The cross of light, symbol of divinity, of the center, the above and the below, the internal fire that gives us the power, that makes us men, and that permits us through resin to consume our tears and offer them in pleasant perfumes to the giver of life."

Notice indeed what it says, "that the perfume of resin, the wind, are intermediaries for us in these ceremonies. The conversations that we are having now, for instance, have to reach Our Lord when we ask him for favors with all our hearts in our own traditions."

The food and fruits represent for us the necessary aliment to aliment the wrapping or the physical body of the spirit. That is for us, for humanity. This kind of vigil is always accompanied by a choral group. Its efforts on behalf of His Highness are designed to implore for kindness for the spirit which leaves matter.

Then, this type of vigil, with the choral group, is for this right now, for us who are here with our armadillo shell performing this ceremony, singing praises to the Lord, venerating him and praising him with appropriate traditions. That is what these things mean, so that no one will misinterpret and [accuse us] of doing other things.

He is God, ritual kin.

He is God.

# C. APPENDICES TO CHAPTER FOUR

## I. PERMISSION (*PERMISO*) TO HOLD A PATRON SAINT FIESTA

The following text is a Spanish and English translation from the original Otomi. The original Otomi with a morpheme-by-morpheme analysis may be found in Lastra (2001:218–226). Today the entire fiesta is carried out in Spanish. That is why we have presented the text in Spanish here. However, in generations past, Otomi was used. The performer of this permission, an Otomi speaker, is no longer living.

> *Señor Santo entierro, Virgen de los Dolores, quien es la dueña de la vida, la dueña de la salud, las benditas animas, me han de ayudar y de acompañar para salir con bien de mi cargo, de mi compromiso. Mi señor del Santo Entierro cruz del Calvario, te pido mucho tu perdón.*
>
> *Dueño de la vida, dueño da la salud. Mi señor, tú me has de ver, tú me has de ayudar. Pido la licencia para salir bien de mi cargo, de mi compromiso. Todas las benditas ánimas que me ayuden y me acompañen. Dueño de la vida dueño, de la salud, pido mi buen camino, mis buenas puertas. Vengo a solicitarte, padre mío señor Santo entierro de la Cruz. Que nos des licencia de salir con bien que te venemos a solicitar permiso. Que sálgamos con bien nosotros de nuestro cargo por todas las benditas animas. Aquellas que dejaron estas tradiciones, aquellas que dejaron estas devociones. Y la Santa Cruz de Palo Huérfano y la Santa Cruz de los padres frailes, la Santa Cruz de la ciudad de Celaya, la Santa Cruz de Acámbaro, la Santa Cruz del cerro de Culiacán, que nos ayude que nos acompañe. Gracias te damos, Santísima Cruz que nos dejates salir con bien en esta fiesta.*
>
> *Santísima Cruz del puerto de Calderón, porque ahí es lo primero, y la Santa Cruz de los Milagros, que es la Santa Cruz de Querétaro, la Santa Cruz del Palo Huérfano, gracias te damos, Santísima Cruz que nos dejates salir con bien en esta fiesta. Gracias te damos, Santísima Cruz, que nos dejates salir con bien a todos tus hijos a toda tu comunidad, ayúdalos, que te vienen a dar las gracias, ayúdalos.*

The Lord Holy Burial, Our Lady of Sorrows, who is the owner of life, the owner of health of the blessed souls, may they help me and accompany me so I will be successful in my duty, my commitment. My Lord Holy Burial Cross of the Calvary, I ask for your pardon.

Owner of life, owner of health. My Lord, you must look after me, you must help me. I ask for permission to be successful in my responsibility, my commitment. May the blessed souls help me and accompany me. Owner of life, owner of health, I ask for a good path, good gates. I come to ask you, my father Lord Holy Burial of the Cross, that you give us permission to do well. We come to ask your permission. That we may do well in our responsibility through the blessed souls. Those who left us these traditions, those who left us these devotions. And the Holy Cross of Palo Huérfano, the Holy Cross of the friars, the Holy Cross of the city of Celaya, the Holy Cross of Acámbaro, the Holy Cross of the mountain of Culiacán, let her help us and accompany us. We give you thanks, most Holy Cross, that you let us come out successfully during this fiesta.

Most Holy Cross of the port of Calderón, because that is the first place, and the Holy Cross of Miracles, who is the Holy Cross of Querétaro, the Holy Cross of Palo Huérfano, we thank you, most Holy Cross, that you permitted us to be successful in this fiesta. We give you thanks, most Holy Cross, that you permitted all of your children in this community, help them, because they come to thank you, help them.

### REFERENCES

Lastra, Yolanda. 2001. *Unidad y diversidad de la lengua: Relatos Otomies.* Mexico City: Instituto de Investigaciones Antropológicas.

### 2. EXCERPTS FROM SPEECHES BY FIESTA OFFICIALS AT THE CHANGING OF DUTIES (*CAMBIO DE CARGOS*), CRUZ DEL PALMAR, JANUARY 1999

*Sabe Dios con qué sacrificio, con qué esfuerzo y con qué lágrimas, porque aquellos señores sí lloraban sus lágrimas, para pedirle a Nuestro Señor su bendición y su socorro, para ayudarnos para que ayudaran a levantar estos cargos que ahoy estamos siguiendo todavía, estos pasos de aquellos antecedentes.*

*Y aquellos que vinieron a implantar esa primera piedra en ese Calvario, aquellos que vinieron a implantar esa primera piedra en esa parroquia que hoy es. Y a los inicios de aquellos entonces que la historia nos dice que era un ranchito pequeño. Su nombre original era Cruz del Palmar. Entonces, a través del tiempo, hemos venido, viendo, esto que todos estamos poco más civilizados en las cosas. Pero a través de eso hay que tener fe en nuestras tradiciones y tenerlo en cuenta que, sí estamos haciendo esto, por intención a las imágenes que están ahí adentro de nuestro templo: el Santo Entierro primeramente, nuestro Padre Jesús y la Virgen de los Dolores. Y a nombre de todas aquellas benditas ánimas del purgatorio, que nos dejaron su santo recuerdo, estamos recordando a traves de este tiempo estos recuerdos. Y tan humildes y tan sencillos, y con aquella fe cristiana. Porque no estamos haciendo otra cosa que no sea en veneración a nuestro Patrón el Santo Entierro, de aquí de esta comunidad, Cruz del Palmar.*

*Ya desde aquí para adelante, seguiremos los pasos y seguiremos nuestras tradiciones como Dios nos dé licencia. Caminaremos estos pasos tanto ustedes esos que no oyen, para que asimismo, vayan agarrando estas tradiciones, y no las dejemos en nuestra comunidad. Entonces, hermanos de la comunidad, pueblo, se puede decir ahoy, de Cruz del Palmar.*

*Y ya les digo, a los inicios, la historia nos está diciendo: en aquellos tiempos era un rancho de Cruz del Palmar. Entonces ahoy ya se va civilizando, ¿verdad? Pero de todas maneras, no porque se está civilizando, vamos a dejar nuestras tradiciones. Yo creo que no es posible porque son unos recuerdos que aquellos antecedentes nos dejaron. Aquellos antepasados nos dejaron para seguir a través de esas lágrimas que ellos lloraron, a través de esos trabajos que ellos dejaron aquí. Y nadien podemos quitar ni nadien podemos poner mano en ninguna de nuestras cosas que ellos nos dejaron. Nuestro es El Calvarito y todo lo que hay en el templo en la parroquia.*

*Entonces, a través de esto que estamos haciendo, de este recuerdo, vamos a seguir con nuestras tradiciones. ¿Qué dicen ustedes? ¿Sí o no?*

*Ave María Purísma.*

Another fiesta official takes over here:

*A nombre de aquellos antecedentes, a nombre de nuestra fe que tenemos, a nombre de las benditas ánimas que dejaron estas santas devociones, porque todo esto que estamos haciendo es un sacrificio, vamos a rezarles un Padre Nuestro.*

God knows what sacrifices, what efforts our ancestors made, and what tears they shed, because those people really cried tears, to ask Our Lord his blessing and his aid, to help us in order to help in the creation of these duties that on this day we are still carrying on, in the steps of those who came before us.

And those who came to lay the first stone in this calvary, and those who came to lay the first stone on this church that is now a parish church. At the beginning history tells us this was a very small settlement. Its original name was Cruz del Palmar. Then, through time, we have come to see that we have become a little more civilized in things. But alongside this we have to have faith in our traditions and bear in mind that if we are doing this, it is because we do it for the images inside our church, first Holy Burial, then Our Father Jesus and Our Lady of Sorrows. And in the name of all the blessed souls in purgatory, who left their holy remembrance, and we remember those memories over time. They were humble and simple, and had Christian faith. Because we are not doing anything except worship our patron saint, Holy Burial, of this community, Cruz del Palmar.

From now on we will follow in their footsteps and we will continue our traditions as long as God gives us permission. We will walk in these footsteps like those of you who no longer hear, so that indeed you go on holding on to our traditions, and do not leave them in this community. Thus, brothers of this community, now we can say village of Cruz del Palmar.

And I am telling you, in the beginning, history tells us: In those times, Cruz del Palmar was a village. Then now it is becoming civilized, right? But in any case, not because it is modernizing should we abandon our traditions. I think it is impossible, because there are memories that those who came before us left us. Those ancestors left traditions for us to continue because of the tears they shed, because of the work they left here. So no one can take away and no one can lay their hands on any of our things they left us. Ours is the little calvary and everything in the parish church.

Then, through what we are doing, because we remember, we will continue our traditions. Don't you agree? Yes or no.

Ave María Purísima.

Another fiesta official takes over here:

In the name of our ancestors, in the name of our faith, in the name of the holy souls who left us these devotions, because what we are doing entails a sacrifice, let us pray to our Father.

### 3. SONG: *ADIÓS, O MADRE MÍA*

*Adiós, reina del cielo,*
*Madre del Salvador.*
*Adiós, o Madre mía,*
*adiós, adiós, adiós.*

*Adiós, reina del cielo,*
*Madre del Salvador,*
*dulce, prenda adorada,*
*de mi sincero amor.*

*De tu divino rostro,*
*la belleza al dejar.*
*Permíteme que vuelva*
*tus plantas a besar.*

*Ah dejarte, o María,*
*no acierta el corazón.*
*Te lo entrego, Señora,*
*dame tu benidición.*

*Adiós, hija del Padre.*
*Madre del hijo, adiós.*
*Del Espíritu Santo*
*o casta esposa, adiós.*

*Adiós, o Madre Virgen,*
*más pura que la luz.*
*Jamás, jamás me olvides,*
*delante de Jesús.*

*Adiós del cielo encanto.*
*Mi delicia y mi amor.*
*Adiós, o Madre mía.*
*Adiós, adiós, adiós.*


Good-bye, queen of heaven,
Mother of the Savior.
Good-bye, o Mother of mine.
Good-bye, good-bye, good-bye.

Good-bye, queen of heaven,
Mother of the Savior,
sweet, adored beloved one,
of my sincere love.

Leaving your divine face,
not looking at its beauty.
Permit me to again
kiss your feet.

My heart, Maria,
cannot leave you.
I give it to you, Lady
Give me your blessing.

Good-bye, daughter of the Father,
Mother of the Son, good-bye.
Chaste wife of the Holy Spirit.
Good-bye.

Good-bye, o Virgin Mother,
purer than light.

Never, never forget me
in front of Jesus.

Good-bye, enchantment of heaven,
my delight and my love.
Good-bye, o Mother of mine.
Good-bye, good-bye, good-bye.

### 4. SONG: *LAS GOLONDRINAS*

*A donde irá, veloz y fatigada,*
*la golondrina que de aquí se va.*
*Por si en el viento se hallara extraviada,*
*buscando abrigo y no lo encontrara.*

*Junto a mi lecho le pondré su nido,*
*en donde pueda la estación pasar.*
*También yo estoy en la región perdido*
*o Cielo Santo! Y sin poder volar.*

*Deje también mi patria idolatrada,*
*esa mansión que me miró nacer.*
*mi vida es hoy errante y angustida,*
*y ya no puedo a mi mansión volver.*

*Ave querida, amada peregrina,*
*mi corazón al tuyo acercaré.*
*Voy recordando, tierna golondrina,*
*recordáre mi patria y lloraré.*

Where will it go, swiftly and tired,
the swallow who is leaving here.
In case it should lose its way in the wind,
looking for shelter and not finding it.

I will put its nest next to my bed
where it can spend the season.
I am also in the lost region
O Holy Heavens! And not able to fly.

I also left my beloved homeland,
that mansion where I was born.

My life today is of wandering and anguish,
and to my mansion I can no longer return.

Dearest bird, beloved pilgrim,
I will draw my heart close to yours.
I go along remembering, sweet swallow,
I will remember my homeland and I will cry.

# D. APPENDIX TO CHAPTER SIX

*El es Dios, Compadre Félix, Compadre Remedios, la Comadrita Lola, y demás comunidades
que vienen de la Cruz del Palmar. Nos ha de dispensar aquí la familia de la comadre Socorro
y en general, que ellos tuvieron la buena voluntad y el cariño de brindarle este comida al padre
Santo Entierro, que viene de la Cruz del Palmar, y por ellos también por ay también a nosotros
nos toca por ay una parte. Pues, esperemos en Dios que las benditas ánimas, todos los santos, y
aquellos que nos dejaron estas tradiciones y estas devociones que nos socorran, que nos bendizcan
donde quiera que estemos, que nos abran nuestras puertas, que no nos falte nuestro pan de cada
día. El venidero, si Él nos presta la vida, pos aquí nos estaremos mirando. Como mucho se dice
para el dos mil, solo Dios sabe qué y qué es lo que vamos a ver para el venidero, solo Dios nuestro
Señor sabe, pero seguiremos, si nos deja nuestro padre Santo Entierro vivir, que nos dé licencia y
fuerza. Pues yo creo que aquí toda la familia Tovares estará con los brazos abiertos esperando a
nuestro padre Santo Entierro y la comunidad de la Cruz del Palmar y todos los de aquí de San
Luis de la Paz. El es Dios, compadritos*
    *El es Dios.*

He is God, Compadre Félix, Comadre Remedios, Comadrita Lola, and the rest of the
community who comes from Cruz del Palmar. The family of the Comadre Socorro here
has to forgive us and in general, these people who had the goodwill and the affection to
offer this meal to the Lord Holy Burial, who comes from Cruz del Palmar, and a part also
comes to us. Well, let us hope in God that the blessed souls, all the saints, and those who
left us these traditions and these devotions will help and bless us wherever we may be,
that they will open the doors for us, that we will not lack our daily bread. Next year, if He
loans us our life, we will be here looking. While much is said about 2000, only God knows
what it is we will see next year, only God knows, but we will continue if our father Holy
Burial permits us to live on, gives us permission and strength. Well, I believe this family
will be here with open arms waiting for our lord Holy Burial and the community of Cruz
del Palmar and all of those from here in San Luis de la Paz. He is God, compadritos.
    He is God.

# NOTES

## INTRODUCTION

1. Jáuregui and Bonfiglioli 1996.

2. Brandes 1988, Ingham 1986.

3. Carmack et al. 1996, Farriss 1984, Foster 1960, García Canclini 1995, Gossen 1993, Gruzinski 1988a, 1988b, 1990, 1999, Ingham 1986, Lockhart 1992, Nahmad 1976, Ricard 1966, Turrent 1993.

4. Carmack et al. 1996, Carrasco 1990, Dow 1896, 1990, Driver and Driver 1963, Galinier 1997, Gossen 1993, Lastra 2000b, 2001, appendix A (this book), León-Portilla 1963, Lockhart 1992, Medina 2000, Uzeta 1998.

5. Alducin Abitia 1986, Bartra 1987, Bonfil Batalla 1996, Lomnitz-Adler 1992, 2001, Merrell 2003, Paz 1961, Ramos 1934.

6. Brandes 1988, Foster 1967.

7. Geertz 1973, Turner 1969.

8. Anderson 1983, Hobsbawm and Ranger 1983. With regard to Latin America, in particular Mexico, see Friedlander (1975) and Urban and Sherzer (1991).

9. García Canclini 1995, Gutierrez 1991, 1993, Harris 2000, Nájera-Ramírez 1997, Rodríguez 1996, Scott 1985, 1990.

10. Bauman 1996, Bauman and Ritch 1994, Hymes 1974, Jáuregui and Bonfiglioli 1996, Sherzer 1983.

11. Bauman 1996, Bauman and Ritch 1994, Becquelin and Breton 2002, Cook 2000, Correa 1997, Harris 2000, Ingham 1986, Jáuregui and Bonfiglioli 1996, Lastra and Nava 2000, Martínez 1998, Monaghan 1990, Nahmad 1976, Nájera-Ramírez 1997, Salvador and Bahm 1982, Uzeta 1998. A very useful bibliography is by Millán et al. (1994).

12. In addition to the appendix to chapter one in this book, Yolanda Lastra has published widely on the languages and cultures of this area (Lastra 1997, 1999a, 1999b, 2000a, 2000b, 2001, 2006a, 2006b; Lastra and Nava 2000).

13. The notion of "deep Mexico" (*México profundo*) is taken from a much discussed book by Bonfil Batalla (1996). He uses the term to refer to the indigenous social and cultural traditions maintained by the peasant and working classes of Mexico, often themselves of indigenous origin. These are the people who participate in the patron saint fiestas

and popular religion we study in this book. See Gandert et al. (2000) and Lamadrid (2003) for a perceptive application to New Mexico.

14. We especially thank Jesus Banca and his wife, Remedios, Ramón Godínez Centeno, Soledad Centeno, Loreto García, Loreto Sanchez Hernández, Cruz Mata, Rosa Morales, Luz Pérez, Antonio Ramírez, Felix Ramírez and his wife, Alexandra, Monico Ramírez and his wife, Sofía, Valente Ramírez and his wife, Braulia, Juan Carlos Rayas, and Refugio Vargas and his wife, Julia. We are also indebted to the numerous people we talked to and whose words appear at different points in this book.

### CHAPTER ONE

1. Schoenhals 1988.

2. Crosses are extremely important in this region. The entire month of May is dedicated to the fiesta of Santa Cruz in various neighborhoods of San Miguel de Allende. There are famous sacred crosses carefully guarded in the countryside. People come from far away to worship them. We are grateful to Phyllis Correa for the many discussions we have had concerning crosses and popular religion more generally in Central Mexico (see also Correa 1997).

3. For a detailed presentation of what went on in this region, see Powell (1952) and Gerhard (1986).

4. In addition to the fiesta of San Luis, there is another traditional fiesta in San Luis de la Paz in honor of the Virgin of Guadalupe. Both Chichimecs and townspeople participate, but not the same ones who participate in the fiesta of San Luis de la Paz.

5. See also Gerhard (1986).

6. Powell 1952.

7. In the San Miguel mission, on the Santa Fe Trail, in Santa Fe, New Mexico, on the old silver route, a continuation of the route in Central Mexico, including Guanajuato, Querétero, and Zacatecas, there is a frieze honoring Saint Louis IX, king of France. It was painted in Mexico in the 1740s and portrays Louis and his wife as great patrons of the Franciscans in the Holy Land. During the seventh and eighth crusades, hospitals, schools, and churches were built. Probably the Franciscan order made the king an honorary member of their order.

8. Gandert et al. 2000, Hale 1996, Lamadrid 2003.

9. See also Lastra (2006b).

10. These dancers are called by various names, according to their imagined or presumed origin (see chapter five and Moedano N. 1981).

11. Lamadrid (2003:4).

### CHAPTER TWO

1. The carguero system has been the subject of a great deal of scholarship because of its significance in Mesoamerica in general and Central Mexico in particular. See, among

others, Brandes (1988), Cancian (1967), Carrasco (1961), Chance (1990), Chance and Taylor (1985), Foster (1967), Greenberg (1981), Monaghan (2000), Mulhare (2000), and Wolf (1959).

2. Correa 1997, Wolf 1958.

3. Gerhard 1986. See also Gruzinski (1988a), Ricard (1966), and Turrent (1993).

4. Albores 1998, Burkhart and Gasco 1996, Farriss 1984.

5. Giffords (1974), in addition to a visual presentation of *retablos,* provides a list of saints honored in Mexico and their attributes.

6. The desert spoon has become an endangered plant through heavy use, and programs exist to replace it, for example in the Charco del Ingenio, an ecological park and botanical garden in San Miguel de Allende.

7. Jáuregui and Bonfiglioli 1996:94.

8. For diagrams of the Four Winds ceremony, see Jáuregui and Bonfiglioli (1996:388).

9. Gruzinski 1990:290.

### CHAPTER THREE

1. León-Portilla 1969, Lord 1960, Sherzer 1990. We are grateful to Robin Moore, who took the time to listen to our recordings of fiesta music and describe their musical structure.

2. Many different interpretations of this mythical feminine figure, La Malinche, exist. In the Matachines dances in New Mexico and elsewhere, Malinche (or the Malinches) are young girls who convert Aztec leaders (Montezuma) to Christianity (Gandert et al, 2000, Jáuregui and Bonfiglioli 1996, Rodriguez 1996). A recent fictional treatment of La Malinche is by Esquivel (2006).

3. Turner 1969. Vigils are widespread in Central Mexico and beyond; we participated in them in various fiestas in Central Mexico and in the fiesta of San Lorenzo in Bernalillo, New Mexico.

### CHAPTER FIVE

1. Jáuregui and Bonfiglioli 1996.

2. These dances are probably of Otomi origin, although the performers usually imagine and construct themselves as Aztecs (Moedano N. 1981). Such groups exist in Texas, Arizona, and California and are associated with particular communities, fiestas, and sometimes schools or museums. For a discussion of concheros in Mexico in general and in Mexico City in particular, see Rostas (1993, 1998).

3. Jáuregui and Bonfiglioli 1996.

4. This procession from house to house to gather food in exchange for music and dancing and the later distribution of the food collected to the community recalls running the Mardi Gras (*courir le Mardi Gras*) in rural Louisiana.

5. Bauman 1996, Bauman and Ritch 1994, Carracedo Navarro n.d.

6. The colors and shapes of hats, and the costumes in general, vary from community to community. In Valle de Maiz the French have yellow caps that recall the hats worn by sixteenth-century Italian nobility. And the Apaches do not wear pants and tunics but a loincloth, and they paint their chests.

### CHAPTER SIX

1. Ingham 1986:1.

2. Guillermo Velázquez Benavides, in May 2006, at the fiesta of the Santa Cruz in the Valle del Maiz neighborhood of San Miguel de Allende. *"Magia y tradición"* is also a song on one of his recordings.

3. Becquelin and Breton 2002:147.

4. We are indebted to John McDowell for goading us into discussing this aspect of patron saint fiestas; he also urged us to refine our position on the relevance of resistance to the study of fiestas.

5. Jáuregui and Bonfiglioli 1996.

6. Turner 1969.

7. Rodríguez 1996:143.

8. Nájera-Castrejón (1995:34) published a picture of an Athapaskan Indian that inspired the Apache dancers in 1933.

9. García Hernández 2002:7–8.

10. Lamadrid 2003:21.

11. Harris 2000, Carrasco Urgoiti 1996.

12. In one of the versions we saw in Cruz del Palmar, this "Indian" was actually the oldest son of the fiesta leader. Battles and wars between Christians and Moors are celebrated in many parts of Europe and Latin America. In Sicily they are narrated by street performers and depicted in performances by large puppets. In Belgium they are also performed by puppets. In northeastern Brazil they are spoken and sung by musicians and singers, and also published in popular booklets hung on clotheslines and therefore called "clothesline literature (*literatura de cordel*) (Pasqualino 1978, Sherzer and Sherzer 1987, Slater 1982). Reenactments of battles between Spaniards and Indians are also found in the Americas, such as the Matachines and Comanche dances of New Mexico (Gandert et al. 2000, Gutierrez 1993, Lamadrid 2003, Rodríguez 1996). In New Mexico, some Matachines dances end with the dancers forming a moving cross and entering the church, thereby symbolically accepting Christianity and rejecting their idolatrous past (Gutierrez 1993). This recalls the carrying of the cross by Indians on the last day of the fiesta in Cruz del Palmar.

13. Moedano N. (1981) The Aztecs are also the object of many fictional accounts that are often quite inventive. See, among others, Azama (1991) and Esquivel (2006).

14. Gutierrez (1991, 1993) and Rodríguez (1996) argue for a counter-hegemonic interpretation of bawdiness and satire in the Matachines dances of New Mexico.

15. May 2005. A year later, in May 2006, Velázquez Benavides used his position as invited itinerant performer and ritual leader to bless the giant puppets, the stilt walker, and the fiesta as a whole. He also entered the church together with the fiesta leader at the head of the procession, before beginning his all-night concert.

16. Wilder 1976:70.

17. Scholars who would view such fiestas in terms of resistance include Beezley, English, and French (1994), García Canclini and Sevilla Villalobos (1985), Gutierrez (1991, 1993), Harris (2000), Nájera-Ramírez (1997), Rodríguez (1996), and Scott (1985, 1990).

18. Bakhtin 1981.

19. Geertz 1973.

20. Childers 2002, Malinowski 1948.

21. This is widespread in Latin America. We are grateful to T. M. Scruggs, an ethnomusicologist who has done research in several Latin American countries, for this information.

22. Farr (2006) describes this phenomenon in detail for Michoacán and among Michoacán migrants in Chicago.

23. Becquelin and Breton 2002, Bricker 1973: photographs following p. 124, Cook 2000, Gandert et al. 2000, Lamadrid 2003, Le Clezio, Rodriguez, and Winningham 1997, Meyer and Beezley 2000 (the photographic essay "Festivals of Mexico" appears after p. 542), Rodríguez 1996 (between pp. 63 and 65), Salvador and Bahm 1982. Jáuregui and Bonfiglioli (1996) provide an excellent set of drawings. For a spectacular exhibit of festivals in indigenous Mexico, see Jackson de Llano (2007–2008).

24. Graburn 1976, Salvador and Bahm 1982.

25. Bricker 1981:179–181, Carrasco 1990:599–600, De la Peña 1980:289, Foster 1967, Galinier 1997, García Canclini 1995, Ingham 1986:7–9, 180–193, Nahmad 1976.

26. Gruzinski 1990:283–294.

27. Ingham 1986:8.

28. Gruzinski 1999:119, Turrent 1993:189. For a description of the elaborate native dances and festivities, see pp. 54–108 in Turrent.

29. Bricker 1986, Stross 1988.

30. Turrent 1993:164–167, 171–172.

31. León-Portilla (1963:32–33) discusses the symbolism associated with the number four for the Aztecs and in another publication (1968:61–65) for the Maya.

32. Gruzinski 1999:113 (translation ours).

33. Gruzinski 1999:113–114 (quoting Bernardino de Sahagún, translation ours).

34. : Galinier 1997:205.

35. Jáuregui and Bonfiglioli 1996:11–12.

36. Ingham 1986:33.

37. Powell 1952.

38. Salvador (1981:58) reports these practices in the Azores.

39. Turrent 1993.

40. Carrasco Urgoiti 1996.

41. Gruzinski 1999:196, Jáuregui and Bonfiglioli 1996:218–210, Monaghan 2000:34–

36. Today, cleansing is performed by plumed dancers, who are reviving and reinventing pre-Hispanic practices.

42. Durán:81.

43. We have benefited from conversations with Kerry Hull and Brian Stross about the complexity of the origins of adorned panels.

44. Phyllis Correa, personal communication. See also Kirchhoff 1947.

45. Sherzer 1983:200–201.

46. Bricker (1973:167–218) elaborates on the cultural and geographic spread of ritual humor.

47. Turrent 1993:154.

48. Gruzinski 1990:274, Salvador and Bahm 1982:55.

49. León-Portilla 1992.

50. Nájera-Castrejón 1995:34.

51. Gillmor 1943.

52. Toor 1947.

53. Wolf 1959:216–218.

54. Ricard 1966.

55. Kurath 1967.

56. *Fiestas in Mexico* 1978.

57. Dow 1990:4, Ingham 1986:48–53, Smith 1975:13.

58. Brenan 1957.

59. Anderson 1983, Hobsbawm and Ranger 1983. With regard to Latin America, see Galinier and Molinié (2006) and Urban and Sherzer (1991). For Mexico in particular, see Friedlander (1975).

60. Powell 1952:39.

61. Anderson 1983, Hobsbawm and Ranger 1983. This fascination with Indianness is widespread, and people capitalize on it. In the summer of 2004 we saw Quechua-speaking Lima residents performing "Amazonian" dances in Lyon, France, in a popular crafts market on a Sunday morning. They were dressed and painted as they imagined Amazonian Indians to be. In Arles, France, that same year we saw other Andean Indians dressed as a combination of Apache and Sioux and singing in Quechua and Spanish. They were also selling their CDs, thus commodifying identity in its expressive form involving costume, music, and dance.

On June 27, 2006, during the soccer world championship game between Brazil and Ghana, when Brazil scored, its supporters stood up and cheered. These were middle-class Brazilians who could afford a trip to Europe for this occasion, yet they were costumed as Amazonian Indians, with painted faces, feathered headdress, and colorful dress. Like plumed dancers in Mexico, these people are constructing themselves as Indians in order to represent, indeed epitomize, Brazil on a world stage.

On July 14, 2006, Bastille Day, in Avignon we observed another construction of Indianness. At night on the main square there were two different groups of Otavalo Indians singing in Quechua and playing Andean music on Andean instruments but costumed as "imagined" Apaches, wearing big Plains Indian headdresses. One of the groups was selling its CD, which was called "Apaches." Here as in Central Mexico we see Apaches (imagined and constructed) representing symbolically the savage American Indian.

62. Ingham 1986.

63. Immigrants, even when far away, because they still feel an allegiance to their patron saints, contribute to the cult of the saints. Fitzgerald (2000) studied a town in Michoacán whose immigrants in the United States raise money for mariachis, flowers, firecrackers, and other costs of their December 5 fiesta. Videos of the fiesta can be purchased in Los Angeles so that viewers can vicariously experience the fiesta. For a while the immigrants also maintained a Web site with a photograph of the fiesta.

# GLOSSARY

*acompañar*   To accompany the saints, for example at vigils and ritual meals.

*alabanza*   Hymn and ballad, sung at all-night vigils.

*ánima*   Soul of the dead, prayed to in cemeteries and visited during processions.

*ánima conquistadora*   Conqueror soul, soul of a dead person who spread Christianity.

*Apache*   Individual costumed as an Apache Indian who appears in dances and dance dramas between French and Apaches.

*atole*   Maize drink consumed at various moments and during various events in fiestas. The word is of Nahuatl origin.

*Azteca*   Individual costumed as an Aztec Indian, represented in plumed dances (also called *conchero*).

*banda*   Brass band, accompanies processions and other events.

*caldo*   Soup, prepared from a slaughtered cow or bull and served to everyone present as part of changing of duties ceremony.

*calvario*   Chapel or niche where people pray, often containing a representation of a saint or a cross.

*cambio de cargos*   Changing of duties from one year's fiesta officials to the next.

*campanita*   Little bell, rung by the female ritual leader, fiesta leader, or other ritual specialist during processions and other ritual events.

*carguero*   Fiesta official.

*castillo*   Castle, a bamboo structure to which are attached various exploding devices that are detonated as part of a nighttime fireworks display.

*Chichimeca*   Indigenous group that has lived in the neighborhood of La Misión in San Luis de la Paz since the eighteenth century. The group has a special relationship with the Otomi-descended population of Cruz del Palmar, with which it has encounters at each other's fiestas.

*chimal*   Adorned panel, other name for *crucero*, also called *súchil* (*súchil* and *chimal* are of Nahuatl origin; *chimal* is the word used in San Luis de la Paz).

*cohete*   Stick rocket, exploded during processions and at other events.

*cohetero*   Stick rocket man, specialist who explodes stick rockets.

*coheton*   Rockets, huge devices that explode loudly.

*comadre*   Ritual godmother who helps fiesta officials in the work they do for the fiesta.

*combate* Combat, term for the final, moving procession of the fiesta in Cruz del Palmar, which occurs in the atrium of the parish church.

*compadrazgo* Ritual kinship system.

*compadre* Ritual godfather who helps fiesta officials in the work they do for the fiesta.

*concha* Lute-like instrument made from an armadillo shell and played during vigils and dances.

*conchero* A player of a *concha,* or a member of a group of plumed dancers one of whom plays the *concha.*

*conquistar* To conquer, convert, and thereby to spread traditions.

*copal* Resin, burned to make perfumed smoke during all-night vigils and other sacred events. The word is of Nahuatl origin.

*coronación* Coronation, official ceremony in which slaves, devotees of the saint, are initiated.

*crucero* (also called *chimal* and *súchil*) Adorned panel (*crucero* is the word used in Cruz del Palmar).

*cuadros* Dance associations.

**Cuatro Vientos** Ceremony of the Four Winds, in which ritual leaders and followers turn in the four cardinal directions. The ceremony is performed to honor a saint and to purify people and places.

*cucharilla* Desert spoon, name of a cactus-like plant used in the construction of altar-pieces and adorned panels.

*cuisillo* Ancient, sacred mound. The word is of Maya origin.

*cumplir* To fulfill one's duties.

*demandita* Doll-like replica of a saint encased in a glass shrine that is carried in processions and encounters and placed on altars during vigils.

*¡Él es dios!* Invocation that recalls the appearance in the sky of the Holy Cross; used to terminate hymns or ballads at all-night vigils and to terminate ritual speeches.

*encuentro* Ritual encounter between two groups.

*esclavos* Slaves, individuals who dedicate themselves to the worship and ritual care of a saint, for example in ritual visits.

*flor y canto* Flower and song, offered to saints at vigils and other events. Expression is a Nahuatl metaphor referring to poetry.

*Francés* Individual costumed as French soldier; appears in dances and dance dramas between French and Apaches.

*huapango* Music-and-dance form consisting of ten-lined rhymed, improvised verses, sometimes performed at fiestas.

*jaripeo* Rodeo.

*limpia* Ritual cleansing or purification that takes place during vigils and other rituals.

*loco* Crazy, cross-dressed and masked satirical and bawdy individual who participates in fiestas.

*manda* Promise to saint to do something for him or her, such as participating in a dance, walking on one's knees in a procession, or committing money for an event, in order to have a request fulfilled.

*mayordomo*   Ritual leader of fiesta, assisted by fiesta officials.

*meco*   Shortened form of *Chichimeco,* used by adolescents.

*mesa*   Table, board, or group of people dedicated to caring for the saints.

*México profundo*   Title of book published by Guillermo Bonfil Batalla in 1996 and meaning "deep Mexico." The term refers to a population of poor, usually indigenous and rural individuals who participate in patron saint fiestas and other aspects of Mexican popular religion.

*mojigangas*   Giant puppets that participate in processions and dance at fiestas.

*Otomi*   Indigenous population located in Central and southern Mexico. Descendents of an Otomi community in Cruz del Palmar have a special relationship with the Chichimecs of San Luis de la Paz, with whom they have encounters at each other's fiestas.

*palabra, la*   "The Word": what people call the resin burner and its smoke.

*palo ensebado*   Greased pole, climbed by young men during fiestas to get gifts at the top.

*papel picado*   Perforated paper (paper cutouts) of different colors used to decorate villages, neighborhoods, and towns during fiestas.

*parande*   Bread board, a wooden frame the size of a bed decorated with cloth or papier maché, from which is hung bread in plastic bags. *Parandes,* like adorned panels, are carried in processions and erected in the atrium of the parish church. Word is of purépecha origin.

*parroquia*   Parish church, term for the main church in a parish, for example in Cruz del Palmar.

*paseo de la vaca*   Promenade of a cow or bull in a procession.

*pasión*   Red flag, carried by female ritual leader in processions.

*permiso*   Ritually requested permission request addressed to God and the saints to hold a fiesta in general and to begin rehearsing for children's dance groups in particular. Involves a procession.

*persignarse*   To cross oneself, also expressed as *hacer se la cruz.*

*pluma, danza de*   Plumed dance, in which dancers are supposed to be dressed as Aztecs. The dancers are also called *concheros.*

*posada*   Ritual visit, especially of saints to houses, where they are cared for by the saint's slaves.

*procession*   Procession.

*ramillete*   Monstrance-like altarpiece made out of desert spoon at vigils, used for blessings.

*recojida de panes*   Gathering of breads, one of many fiesta processions.

*reliquia*   Ritual meal, held at various moments during fiestas.

*rosa*   Ritual paraphernalia carried by the female ritual leader in processions and elsewhere. The items include a small bell, a red flag (*pasión*), candles, and other ritual objects. This term is not used everywhere.

*sahumar*   To perfume with resin at vigils and in processions and encounters.

*sahumador*   Resin burner used at vigils and in processions and encounters.

*santo, santito*   What saints are called when represented as *demandita.*

*San Luisito*  Saint Louis, patron saint of San Luis de la Paz. The saint's day is August 25. Often called San Luis Rey or San Luisito.

*Santo Entierro*  Holy Burial, patron saint of Cruz del Palmar. The saint's day is January 1.

*sonaja, danza de*  Rattle dance. Children wearing straw hats decorated with paper flowers dance to the sound of violins and trumpets while shaking tin rattles (*sonajas*), which give the dance its name.

*súchil*  One of the terms for adorned panel (see *crucero*). Word is of Nahuatl origin.

*tejer*  To weave; term used in the making of altarpieces and adorned panels, as in weaving desert spoon into the frame.

*tenancha*  Female ritual leader who leads processions and participates ritually in vigils carrying a red flag and ringing a little bell. Word is of Nahuatl origin (*te-nan-tzin* means one's dear mother).

*torito*  Small representation of a bull that, like *castillo,* is exploded as fireworks. It is handheld and is used to playfully frighten children.

*torito, baile de*  Dance of the bulls. A playful, humorous imitation bullfight with individuals inside puppet-like or body-mask bulls, performed at fiestas.

*velación*  Vigil (usually lasting all night).

*zanco*  Stilt. People on stilts appear in fiesta processions.

# REFERENCES

Albores, Beatriz. 1998. Los otomianos del Alto Lerma mexiquense: Un enfoque etnoló-
gico. *Estudios de Cultura Otopame* 1:187–214.

Alducin Abitia, Enrique. 1986. *Los Valores de los Mexicanos*. Mexico City: Banamex.

Anderson, Benedict. 1983. *Imagined communities: Reflections on the origin and spread of
nationalism.* London: Verso.

Azama, Michel 1991. *Aztèques*. Paris: Éditions Theatrales.

Bakhtin, Mikail M. 1981. *The dialogic imagination.* Austin: University of Texas Press.

Bartra, Roger. 1987. *La jaula de la melancolia.* Mexico City: Grijalbo.

Bauman, Richard. 1996. Transformations of the word in the production of Mexican festival drama. In *Natural histories of discourse,* ed. Michael Silverstein and Greg Urban,
301–327. Chicago: University of Chicago Press.

Bauman, Richard, and Pamela Ritch. 1994. Informing performance: Producing the *coloquio* in Tierra Blanca. *Oral Tradition* 9(2):255–280.

Becquelin, Aurore Monod, and Alain Breton. 2002. *La "guerre rouge" ou une politique Maya
du sacré: Un carnaval Tzeltal au Chipas, Mexique.* Paris: CNRS Editions.

Beezley, William H., Cheryl English, and William E. French, eds. 1994. *Rituals of rule,
rituals of resistance: Public celebrations and popular culture in Mexico.* Wilmington, Del.:
Scholarly Resources.

Bonfil Batalla, Guillermo. 1996. *México profundo: Reclaiming a civilization.* Austin: University of Texas Press.

Brandes, Stanley. 1988. *Power and persuasion: Fiestas and social control in rural Mexico.*
Philadelphia: University of Pennsylvania Press.

Brenan, Gerald. 1957. *South from Granada.* New York: Farrar, Strauss and Cudahy.

Bricker, Victoria Reifler. 1973. *Ritual humor in highland Chiapas.* Austin: University of
Texas Press.

———. 1981. *The Indian Christ, the Indian king: The historical substrate of Maya myth and
ritual.* Austin: University of Texas Press.

———. 1986. *A grammar of Maya hieroglyphs.* New Orleans: Middle American Research
Institute, Tulane University.

Burkhart, Louise M., and Janine Gasco. 1996. The colonial period in Mesoamerica. In
*The legacy of Mesoamerica: History and culture of a Native American civilization,* ed.

Robert M. Carmack, Janine Gasco, and Gary H. Gossen, 154–195. Saddle River, N.J.: Prentice Hall.

Cancian, Frank. 1967. Political and religious organizations. In *Handbook of Middle American Indians,* vol. 6, ed.Robert Wauchope and Manning Nash, 283–298. Austin: University of Texas Press.

Carmack, Robert M., Janine Gasco, and Gary H. Gossen. 1996. *The legacy of Mesoamerica: History and culture of a Native American civilization.* Upper Saddle River, N.J.: Prentice Hall.

Carracedo Navarro, David M. n.d. *Del huapango arribeño te cuento risueño.* Querétaro, Mexico: Unidad Regional de Culturas Populares.

Carrasco, Davíd. 1990. *Religions of Mesoamerica: Cosmovision and ceremonial centers.* New York: Harper and Row.

Carrasco, Pedro. 1961. The civil-religious hierarchy in Meso American communities: Pre-Spanish background and colonial development. *American Anthropologist* 63(4):483–497.

Carrasco Urgoiti, María Soledad. 1996. *El moro retador y el moro amigo: Estudios sobre fiestas y comedias de moros y cristianos.* Granada, Spain: University of Granada.

Chance, John K. 1990. Changes in twentieth-century Meso-american cargo systems. In *Class, politics, and popular religion in Mexico and Central America,* ed. Lynn Stephen and James Dow, 27–42. Washington, D.C.: American Anthropological Association.

Chance, John K., and William B. Taylor. 1985. Cofradias and cargos: A historical perspective on the Mesoamerican civil religious hierarchy. *American Ethnologist* 12(1):1–26.

Childers, William. 2002. Chicanoizing Don Quixote: For Luis Andrés Murillo. *Aztlán* 27(2):87–117.

Cook, Garrett, W. 2000. *Renewing the Maya world: Expressive culture in a highland town.* Austin: University of Texas Press.

Correa, Phyllis M. 1997. La religión popular en el estado de Guanajuato: El culto a la Santa Cruz del Puerto de Calderón. *Revista Mexicana de Estudio Antropológicos* 43:69–88.

De la Peña, Guillermo. 1980. *Herederos de promesas: Agricultura, política y ritual en los altos de Morelos.* Mexico City: Centro de Investigaciones Superiores del Instituto Nacional de Antropología e Historia.

Dow, James W. 1986. *The shaman's touch: Otomí Indian symbolic healing.* Salt Lake City: University of Utah Press.

———. 1990. *Santos y supervivencias.* Mexico City: Instituto Nacional Indigenista.

Driver, Harold, and Wilhelmine Driver. 1963. *Ethnography of the Chichimeco-Jonaz of northeast Mexico.* Bloomington: Indiana University Research Center in Anthropology, Folklore, and Linguistics, publication 26, IJAL 29, no. t, pt. II.

Durán, fray Diego. 1983. *Book of the gods and rites: The ancient calendar.* Norman: University of Oklahoma Press.

Esquivel, Laura. 2006. *Malinche.* New York: Atria Books.

Farr, Marcia. 2006. *Rancheros in Chicagoacán: Language and identity in a transnational community.* Austin: University of Texas Press.

Farriss, Nancy. 1984. *Maya society under colonial rule: The collective enterprise of survival.* Princeton, N.J.: Princeton University Press.

*Fiestas in Mexico.* 1978. *Fiestas in Mexico: A complete guide to celebrations throughout the country.* Mexico City: Ediciones Lara.

Fitzgerald, David. 2000. *Negotiating extra-territorial citizenship: Mexican migration and the transnational politics of community.* CCIS monograph 2. La Jolla: University of California, San Diego.

Foster, George M. 1960. *Culture and conquest: America's Spanish heritage.* New York: Wenner-Gren Foundation for Anthropological Research.

———. 1967. *Tzintzuntzan: Mexican peasants in a changing world.* Boston: Little, Brown.

Friedlander, Judith. 1975. *Being Indian in Hueyapan: A study of forced identity in contemporary Mexico.* New York: St. Martin's Press.

Galinier, Jacques. 1997. *La moitié du monde: Le corps et le cosmos dans de rituel des indiens Otomí.* Paris: PUF.

Galinier, Jacques, and Antoinette Molinié. 2006. *Les Néo Indiens: Une religion du IIIe millenaire.* Paris: Odile Jacob.

Gandert, Miguel, Enrique R. Lamadrid, Ramón A. Gutiérrez, Lucy R. Lipard, and Chris Wilson. 2000. *Nuevo México Profundo: Rituals of an Indo-Hispano homeland.* Santa Fe: Museum of New Mexico Press.

García Canclini, Néstor. 1995. *Hybrid cultures: Strategies for entering and leaving modernity.* Minneapolis: University of Minnesota Press.

García Canclini, Néstor, and Amparo Sevilla Villalobos. 1985. *Máscaras, danzas y fiestas de Michoacán.* Mexico City: Impresora Publicataria y Editorial.

García Hernández, Jose Omar. 2002. Nuestra Historia. http://www.sanluisdelapaz.com/cmsystem/index.php?categoryid=10.

Geertz, Clifford. 1973. *The interpretation of cultures.* New York: Basic Books.

Gerhard, Peter. 1986. *Geografía histórica de la Nueva España 1519–1821.* Mexico City: Universidad Nacional Autónoma de México.

Giffords, Gloria Kay. 1974. *Mexican folk retablos: Masterpieces on tin.* Tucson: University of Arizona Press.

Gillmor, Frances. 1943. *The dance dramas of Mexican villages.* Tucson: University of Arizona Press.

Gossen, Gary H., ed. 1993. *South and Meso-American native spirituality: From the cult of the feathered serpent to the theology of liberation.* New York: Crossroad Publishing.

Graburn, Nelson H. H., ed. 1976. *Ethnic and tourist arts: Cultural expressions from the fourth world.* Berkeley and Los Angeles: University of California Press.

Greenberg, James B. 1981. *Santiago's sword: Chatino peasant religion and economics.* Berkeley and Los Angeles: University of California Press.

Gruzinski, Serge. 1988a. *La colonization de l'imaginaire: Sociétés indigenes et occidentalisation dans le Mexique espagnol, XVIe–XVIIIe siècle.* Paris: Gallimard.

———. 1988b. *Le destin brisé de l'empire Aztèque.* Paris: Gallimard.

———. 1990. *La guerre des images.* Paris: Gallimard.

———. 1999. *La pensée métisse.* Paris: Fayard.

Gutierrez, Ramon. 1991. *When Jesus came, the corn mothers went away.* Stanford, Calif.: Stanford University Press.

———. 1993. The politics of theater in colonial New Mexico: Drama and the rhetoric of conquest. In *Reconstructing a Chicano/a literary heritage,* ed. María Herrera-Sobek, 49–67. Tucson: University of Arizona Press.

Hale, Charles R. 1996. *Mestizaje,* hybridity, and the cultural politics of difference in post-revolutionary Central America. *Journal of Latin American Anthropology* 2(1):34–61.

Harris, Max. 2000. *Aztecs, Moors, and Christians: Festivals of reconquest in Mexico and Spain.* Austin: University of Texas Press.

Hobsbawm, Eric, and Terrence Ranger, eds. 1983. *The invention of tradition.* Cambridge: Cambridge University Press.

Hymes, Dell. 1974. *Foundations in sociolinguistics: An ethnographic approach.* Philadelphia: University of Pennsylvania Press.

Ingham, John. 1986. *Mary, Michael, and Lucifer: Folk Catholicism in Central Mexico.* Austin: University of Texas Press.

Jackson de Llano, George O. Sept.26, 2007–Apr. 15, 2008. *Mexican cycles: Festival images.* Exhibit at the Museum of Natural History, Smithsonian Institution. www.mnh.si.edu/exhibits/cycles/index_eng.html.

Jáuregui, Jesús, and Carlo Bonfiglioli, coords. 1996. *Las danzas de conquista.* Vol. I. *México contemporáneo.* Mexico City: Fondo de Cultura Económica.

Kirchhoff, Paul. 1947. La historia Tolteca-Chichimeca: Un estudio histórico-sociológico. In *Historia Tolteca chichimeca: Anales de Quauhtinchan.* Version prepared and annotated by Heinrich Berlin in collaboration with Silvia Rendón, xix–liv. Mexico City: Antigua Librería Robredo de José Porrúa e hijos.

Kurath, Gertrude Prokosch. 1967. Drama, dance, and music. In *Handbook of Middle American Indians,* vol. 6, ed. Robert Wauchope and Manning Nash, 158–190. Austin: University of Texas Press.

Lamadrid, Enrique R. 2003. *Hermanitos comanchitos: Indo-Hispano rituals of captivity and redemption.* Albuquerque: University of New Mexico Press.

Lastra, Yolanda. 1997. El español rural de San Miguel Allende, Guanajuato. In *Varia lingüística y literaria,* ed. Rebeca Barriga Villanueva and Pedro Martín Butragueño, 480–489. Mexico City: El Colegio de México.

———. 1999a. Rasgos otomíes en el español rural de San Miguel Allende, Guanajuato. In *Homenaje a Rafael Torres Quintero,.* Thesaurus LII (1997), 206–212. Bogota: Instituto Caro y Cuervo.

———. 1999b. Testimonios del habla de San Luis de la Paz, Guanajuato. *Español Actual,* no. 71, 63–71.

———. 2000a. ¿Es el otomí una lengua amenazada? *Anales de Antropología,* vol. 33 (1996–1999), IIA, 361–396. Mexico City: Universidad Nacional Autónoma de México.

———. 2000b. Lenguaje, cultura e identidad entre los grupos otomianos del estado de Guanajuato. *Estudios de Cultura Otopame* 2:147–162.

———. 2001. *Unidad y diversidad de la lengua: Relatos otomíes*. Mexico City: Instituto de Investigaciones Antropológicas, Universidad Nacional Autónoma de México.

———. 2006a. *Los Otomíes: Su lengua y su historia*. Mexico City: Instituto de Investigaciones Antropológicas, Universidad Nacional Autónoma de México.

———. 2006b. El léxico de la religión popular en el área de San Miguel de Allende. In *Homenaje a José Moreno de Alba,* ed. Company Concepción, 317–331. Mexico City: Instituto de Investigaciones Filológicas, Universidad Nacional Autónoma de México.

Lastra, Yolanda, and Fernando Nava. 2000. La fiesta de la Santa Cruz del Valle del Maíz. *Estudios de Cultura Otopame* 2:163–178.

Lavenda, Robert H. 1986. Festivals and carnivals. In *Handbook of Latin American Popular Culture,* ed. Harold E. Hinds, Jr., and Charles M. Tatum, 191–205. Westport, Conn.: Greenwood Press.

Le Clezio, J.M.G., Richard Rodriguez, and Geoff Winningham. 1997. *In the eye of the sun: Mexican fiestas*. New York: W. W. Norton.

León-Portilla, Miguel. 1963. *Aztec thought and culture*. Norman: University of Oklahoma Press.

———. 1969. *Pre-Columbian literatures of Mexico*. Norman: University of Oklahoma Press.

———. 1988. *Time and reality in the thought of the Maya*. Norman: University of Oklahoma Press.

León-Portilla, Miguel, ed. 1992. *Visión de los vencidos. Relaciones indígenas de la conquista*. Mexico City: Universidad Nacional Autónoma de México.

Lockhart, James. 1992. *The Nahuas after the conquest*. Stanford, Calif.: Stanford University Press.

Lomnitz-Adler, Claudio. 1992. *Exit from the labyrinth: Culture and ideology in the Mexican national space*. Berkeley and Los Angeles: University of California Press.

———. 2001. *Deep Mexico, silent Mexico: An anthropology of nationalism*. Minneapolis: University of Minnesota Press.

Lord, Albert B. 1960. *The singer of tales*. Cambridge, Mass.: Harvard University Press.

Malinowski, Bronislaw. 1948. *Magic, science and religion and other essays*. Garden City, N.Y.: Doubleday Anchor.

Martínez, Herón Pérez, ed. 1998. *México en fiesta*. Zamora, Michoacán, Mexico: Colegio de Michoacán.

Medina, Andrés. 2000. *En las cuatro esquinas, en el centro: Etnografía de la cosmovisión mesoamericana*. Mexico City: Universidad Nacional Autónoma de México.

Merrell, Floyd. 2003. *The Mexicans: A sense of culture*. Cambridge: Westview Press.

Meyer, Michael, and William H. Beezley, eds. 2000. *The Oxford history of Mexico*. Oxford: Oxford University Press.

Millán, Saúl, Miguel Ángel Rubio, and Andrés Ortiz. 1994. *Fiestas de los pueblos indígenas: Historia y etnografía de la fiesta en México. Bibliografía general*. Mexico City: Instituto Nacional Indigenista.

Moedano N., Gabriel. 1981. La danza de los concheros de Querétaro. In *Problemas del*

*Desarrollo Histórico de Querétaro,* ed. Margarita Velasco. Querétaro: Editora Offset Color.

Monaghan, John D. 1990. Reciprocity, redistribution, and the transaction of value in the Mesoamerican fiesta. *American Ethnologist* 17(4):758–744.

————. 2000. Theology and history in the study of Mesoamerican religions. In *Supplement to Handbook of Middle American Indians,* vol. 6, ed. John D. Monaghan, 24–49. Austin: University of Texas Press.

Mulhare, Eileen M. 2000. Mesoamerican social organization and community after 1960. In *Supplement to Handbook of Middle American Indians,* vol. 6, ed. John D. Monaghan, 9–23. Austin: University of Texas Press.

Nahmad, Solomon. 1976. Mexican feasts: Syncretism and cultural identity. *Cultures* 3(2):45–58.

Nájera-Castrejón, Francisco. 1995. Los "Diablos" de Teloloapan: Leyenda Costumbrista. Teloloapan, Guerrero, Mexico: Museo Municipal "Gral. Jesús H. Salgado."

Nájera-Ramírez, Olga. 1997. *La fiesta de los Tastoanes: Critical encounters in Mexican festival performance.* Albuquerque: University of New Mexico Press.

Pasqualino, Antonio. 1978. *L'Opera dei pupi.* Palermo: Sellerio Editore.

Paz, Octavio. 1961. *The labyrinth of solitude: Life and thought in Mexico.* New York: Grove Press.

Powell, Philip Wayne. 1952. *Soldiers, Indians and silver: The northward advance of New Spain, 1550–1600.* Berkeley and Los Angeles: University of California Press.

Ramos, Samuel. 1934. *El perfil del hombre.* Mexico City: Imprenta Mundial.

Ricard, Robert. 1966. *The spiritual conquest of Mexico.* Berkeley and Los Angeles: University of California Press.

Rodríguez, Sylvia. 1996. *The Matachines dance: Ritual symbolism and interethnic relations in the upper Río Grande Valley.* Albuquerque: University of New Mexico Press.

Rostas, Susanna. 1993. The *Mexica's* reformulation of the Concheros' dance: The popular use of autochthonous religion in Mexico City. In *The popular use of popular religion in Latin America,* ed. Susanna Rostas and André Droogers, 211–224. Amsterdam: CEDLA.

————. 1998. From ritualization to performativity: The concheros of Mexico. In *Ritual, performance, media,* ed. Felicia Hughes Freeland, 85–103. ASA Monograph 35. London: Routledge.

Salvador, Mari Lyn. 1981. *Portuguese religious celebrations in the Azores and California.* Oakland, Calif.: Oakland Museum History Department.

Salvador, Mari Lyn, and Linda Bahm. 1982. *Fiestas of San Juan Nuevo: Ceremonial art from Michoacán, Mexico.* Albuquerque, N.M.: Maxwell Museum of Anthropology.

Schoenhals, Louise C. 1988. *Spanish-English glossary of Mexican flora and fauna.* Mexico City: Summer Institute of Linguistics.

Scott, James C. 1985. *Weapons of the weak: Everyday forms of peasant resistance.* New Haven, Conn.: Yale University Press.

————. 1990. *Domination and the arts of resistance.* New Haven, Conn.: Yale University Press.

Sherzer, Joel. 1983. *Kuna ways of speaking: An ethnographic perspective*. Austin: University of Texas Press.

———. 1990. *Verbal art in San Blas: Kuna culture through its discourse*. Cambridge: Cambridge University Press.

Sherzer, Joel, and Dina Sherzer, eds. 1987. *Humor and comedy in puppetry: Celebration in popular culture*. Bowling Green, Oh.: Popular Press.

Slater, Candace. 1982. *Stories on a string: The Brazilian literature de cordel*. Berkeley and Los Angeles: University of California Press.

Smith, Robert. 1975. *The art of the festival*. University of Kansas Publications in Anthropology 6. Lawrence, Kan.

Stross, Brian. 1988. The burden of office: A reading. *Mexicon* 10:118–121.

Toor, Frances. 1947. *A treasury of Mexican folkways: The customs, myths, folklore, traditions, beliefs, fiestas, dances and songs of the Mexican people*. New York: Crow Publishers.

Turner, Victor. 1969. *The ritual process: Structure and anti-structure*. Ithaca, N.Y.: Cornell University Press.

Turrent, Lourdes. 1993. *La conquista musical de México*. Mexico City: Fondo de Cultura Económica.

Urban, Greg, and Joel Sherzer, eds. 1991. *Nation-states and Indians in Latin America*. Austin: University of Texas Press.

Uzeta, Jorge. 1998. La fiesta de San Luis Rey: Unidad y fragmentación popular en un ritual religioso. *Regiones* 9 (enero-junio): 121–142. CICSUG, Universidad de Guanajuato.

Wilder, Mitchell A. 1976. *Santos: The religious folk art of New Mexico*. New York: Hacker Art Book.

Wolf, Eric. 1958. The virgin of Guadalupe: A Mexican national symbol. *Journal of American Folklore* 71:34–39.

———. 1959. *Sons of the shaking earth*. Chicago: University of Chicago Press.

# INDEX

LaVergne, TN USA
22 January 2011
213553LV00003B/5/P